Artistry in Teaching

Louis J. Rubin

University of Illinois at Urbana-Champaign

McGraw-Hill, Inc.
New York St. Louis San Francisco Auckland Bogotá
Caracas Lisbon London Madrid Mexico Milan
Montreal New Delhi Paris San Juan Singapore
Sydney Tokyo Toronto

Teaching may be compared to selling commodities. No one can sell unless someone buys. We should ridicule a merchant who said that he had sold a great many goods although no one had bought any. But perhaps there are teachers who think they have done a good day's teaching irrespective of what pupils have learned.

—John Dewey

ARTISTRY IN TEACHING

First Edition

987654

Library of Congress Cataloging in Publication Data

Rubin, Louis J.
    Artistry in teaching.

    Includes index.
    1. Teaching. 2. Teachers—Psychology. 3. Creative thinking (Education) 4. Motivation in education. 5. Learning. I. Title.
LB1025.2.R735   1984   371.1'02   84-11771
ISBN 0-07-554606-X

Cover Design: Sharon Glassman.
Photo Credits: Page 12: Josephus Daniels/Rapho-Photo Researchers; page 96: Cary Wolinsky/Stock, Boston.

PREFACE

Artistry in Teaching is written for those who are in education programs today and who will be teachers tomorrow. It is especially for those teachers-in-training who believe teaching can be an art, and whose aim is to make themselves Artist Teachers. It is for all who remember the teacher who once inspired them, and for those same people concerned now about the quality of instruction in our schools. It is for those who want their teaching to make a difference.

The quality of teaching in the nation's schools has again come to the forefront of public concern. Critic after critic has alluded to instructional weaknesses in the educational system. The criticisms decry the lackluster performance of teachers, the narrow range of teaching methods, the boredom of classrooms, and the seeming ineptness of teacher training.

Notable deficiencies do indeed exist. Few beginning teachers, for example, regard their pre-service preparation as adequate. Principals echo this sentiment, noting that first-year teachers neither know enough about what they are to teach, nor about how it should be taught. These problems are hardly new. Reasonable solutions, moreover, exist. The difficulties, unhappily, seem to lie in the bureaucratic impediments of the system itself. Recently, for example, I was asked by a training institution to suggest desirable revisions. The recommendations were far from earth-shattering:

1. A more rigorous selection of teacher training candidates, even at the risk of creating a future shortage.
2. A higher concentration, in pre-service training, on liberal arts courses—with specific emphasis upon intellectual concepts related to the instructional curriculum.
3. A reduction in pre-service methods courses, coupled with primary stress upon generic teaching skills: organizing, pacing, questioning, motivating, evaluating, and so on.
4. A careful coordination of field training experiences with the re-

quired methods courses. Teaching techniques, taught in methods courses, should be practiced, simultaneously, in a real-world situation.

5. Utilizing supervising teachers in field training who are themselves excellent practitioners, modeling teaching at its best.

6. Placing graduates—trained in the above manner—in schools which are willing to perpetuate the development of potentially outstanding teachers.

7. Continuing the training of these graduates through apprenticeship programs in schools.

Once they go to work, teachers eventually become somewhat more adept, mainly by imitating those who have been around longer and by experimenting, through trial and error, until something works. Their in-service training—designed to keep them abreast of changing events and to refine their skills—is, as a rule, not much better than their earlier training.

Of late, there also has been a growing teacher resentment over the increasingly prescriptive nature of their professional growth programs. More and more, teachers are coming to be viewed as mindless robots who are expected to carry out the dictates of someone with superior judgment. As a result, personal commitment has given way to listless rule-following. In a recent book, Milton and Rose Friedman comment on the trend toward conformity:

> In our view, the financial reason for the deterioration of schooling is increasing centralization and bureaucratization of public schooling. This is a process that has been going on since early in the century, but it accelerated after the 1930s. The number of school districts declined from about 128,000 in 1932 to 84,000 by 1950, and to 16,000 by 1980. Both control and financing of schooling have been transferred from local communities to large school districts, and then to state departments of education, and recently more and more to the federal government. Professional educators—not parents or students—have increasingly decided what should be taught, how, by whom, and to whom. Monopoly and uniformity have replaced competition and diversity. Control by producers has replaced control by consumers.*

Whether or not one agrees with the Friedmans' economic arguments, it would be hard to deny that centralization has heavily

---

* Milton and Rose Friedman, *Tyranny of the Status Quo* (New York: Harcourt Brace Jovanovich, 1984), pp. 152–53.

damaged individual incentive. This book, in considerable degree, is addressed to the premise that teachers must find their own identity. Doing so, however, has become increasingly difficult as conditions have deteriorated. It is not merely a matter of larger classes, fewer supplies, and insufficient provisions for students prone to disruptive behavior—the work environment itself has become harsh and dispirited.

Professional malaise, as a result, is very great. Young people of talent are choosing other careers; the best and brightest of those who do enter teaching are the first to leave, and those who remain are further depressed by discordant complaints that lack consensual values.

The book, it should be said, is not a quick antidote. Improvements in our educational system will not come easily. But there are still great teachers, who inspire students and who have elevated teaching to a fine art. *Artistry in Teaching* describes the characteristics, attributes, beliefs, and inner discipline of such teachers. The result of a long study, it focuses, not on teaching methods, but rather on the factors that give methods vitality and force. Contrary to popular assumption, no teaching technique—however good it may be—is fail-proof. The supporting factors, in fact, are so powerful that they often produce excellent learning, even when the basic method is faulty.

There is a striking quality to fine classrooms. Students are caught up in the learning; excitement abounds; and playfulness and seriousness blend easily because the purposes are clear, the goals sensible, and an unmistakable feeling of well-being prevails.

Artist teachers achieve these qualities by knowing both their subject matter and their students; by guiding the learning with deft control—a control that itself is born out of perception, intuition, and creative impulse. The ways in which these invigorate and fortify basic instructional methods are illustrated by a series of capsule vignettes which appear throughout the book. The vignettes were necessary because artistic teaching must be illustrated and described, rather than encapsulated in a recipe.

Intended for teachers, both pre-service and practicing, supervisors, principals, parents, and school board members, *Artistry in Teaching* is not another recital of ancient proverbs about how to teach. Nor does it offer a few simple steps for raising test scores. What it does, instead, is:

1. Show the myriad ways in which students can be motivated

2. Describe how teacher-induced drama can alleviate habitual class-room tedium
3. Illustrate the importance of teacher improvisation
4. Demonstrate devices through which teachers can create an atmosphere conducive to learning
5. Reveal the "performance" aspects of teaching
6. Stress that each teacher must develop a natural style out of personal aptitudes and skills
7. Suggest that fine teaching, which stimulates children's intellectual growth, carries its own intrinsic rewards
8. Give examples of how intuitive thinking can facilitate teacher effectiveness
9. Unveil some of the mysteries surrounding teacher charisma
10. Contend that teaching is a vocation worthy of high celebration

For these, and other, reasons, it is to be hoped that a reading of the book will prove to be both valuable and time well-spent.

Some endeavors take longer than others. The volume suffered, for an assortment of reasons, repeated interruptions, and was six years in gestation. In the spring of 1978 I presented a paper, outlining the major conceptions, at the annual meeting of the Association for Supervision and Curriculum Development in San Francisco. I asked Elliot W. Eisner to critique the manuscript. Later that summer, while at Stanford, I discussed the concepts with Nathaniel Gage, who was then doing a book of his own on teaching.

During the intervening years, a number of people offered encouragement and valuable advice. Philip Hosford gave helpful suggestions after the San Francisco presentation; Selma Wasserman provided a perceptive critique of the first draft; Sandra Boulanger recommended a useful reorganization of the material; Larry Colker enlarged my frame of reference; Sister Judine prodded when necessary; Cynthia Mitchell assisted with structural details; June Chambliss and her co-workers performed magic with a word processor; Loretta Giorcelli facilitated some of the revisions; and Veronica Stephen helped it all come together.

This book is aimed at those interested in the art and science of teaching. The principal themes are that our present system of teacher preparation cannot produce outstanding practitioners; that great teachers fashion a personal style around their educational convictions; that imagination and inventiveness are far more important than standard operating procedures; and that a passion for enlightening young minds is the driving force behind master teachers.

Louis J. Rubin

CONTENTS

Artistry in Teaching

PROLOGUE:
TEACHING AND
LEARNING

This is a book about teaching. Over the years, much has been written about the subject. Beyond the massive amount of formal research, there has been an endless array of opinion, conjecture, and testimonial. Most of the writing, however, has dealt with teaching methods and the content of learning—with the substance of what is taught and how it is taught. These, obviously, are of great importance. But there also are other aspects of the teaching art, perhaps equally important, which appear to have received little or no attention.

There has been a tendency to assume that the right subject matter, taught in the right way, will produce classrooms that work effectively. Experience, alas, has proved otherwise. For example, it has been popular recently to fault lecture and discussion as teaching techniques. Neither of these, critics contend, is as beneficial as heuristic procedures through which students explore unknowns and learn by solving problems. It could be demonstrated that some of the best—and worst—teachers regularly employ both methods. We sometimes confuse the method with the spirit. Good teaching materials and efficient techniques are not enough: Why is it, for example, that two classrooms—in which the teachers use essentially the same methods and materials—are nonetheless strikingly different? What accounts for the fact that some classes are exciting and others dreary? Why do students react to one teacher with delight and to another with disdain, despair, or dread?

The difference apparently lies in the intangibles of artistry—the skillfulness of the teaching. These intangibles transcend charisma, although gifted teachers often are blessed with charismatic qualities. Pedagogical excellence often goes beyond conventional form because artistic teachers neither act in precisely the same way nor embrace uniform beliefs about the purposes of teaching. Similarly, there is no proven direct correlation between teacher intelligence and skillful teaching, or between knowledgeability and pedagogical adeptness. Highly successful teachers, obviously, are neither uninformed nor halfwitted. Their effectiveness, however, is as attributable to "people smarts" as to "book smarts," and they achieve impressive results through an amalgam of skills which almost literally "make the student learn." These intangibles also involve passion and a powerful desire to excel. But commitment, while essential, is but one element in the formula: highly dedicated teachers often obtain only meager results. Nor is artistry entirely dependent upon humanistic impulse and personal warmth. Gifted teachers, upon occasion, are relatively authoritarian in their approach. The qualities which undergird teaching virtuosity, in short, are elusive precisely because they are difficult to analyze and describe. Yet, they exist.

Experienced classroom observers readily agree that teachers favor different styles. Style—in this context—is not a matter of whether teachers use objective or essay tests, rely predominantly on lecture or discussion, or assign homework. Rather, it has to do with the approach teachers use in pursuing their purposes.

Even when using similar methodologies and content, teachers vary considerably in the way they deal with students. Their teaching styles invariably reflect their personalities. The behavior they favor, the attitudes they seek to instill, and the insights they strive to develop in their students often differ from practitioner to practitioner, even when each uses the same text and follows the same course of study. Moreover, they frequently attack an objective through widely disparate procedures. One teacher rules with a heavy hand, and another with a light touch; some entreat while others mandate; and what is prized in one classroom may be prohibited in another. Such inconsistencies are dramatically illustrated in the oft-cited example where five teachers, asked to grade the same English composition, assign grades which range from a C− to an A.

Since style has its roots in personality and belief, the artistic embellishments in a teacher's performance must fit his or her nature. Thus, every practitioner evolves a personalized set of procedures. Artistic techniques, in short, cannot be transplanted at will. Each teacher, must, in one way or another, develop a collection of devices which work.

Two facts, in the main, distinguish the strong teachers from the weak: they manage whatever techniques they use with great skill—that is, they are able to use a device expertly, so that its usefulness is maximized—and they utilize these skills in appropriate contexts. How well a teaching strategy is used, apparently, may make more difference than the strategy itself. This "feel" for the right thing at the right time is the benchmark of expertness.

Whether or not such skills are learnable is uncertain. There are those who contend that the ability to motivate others is a natural endowment, a kind of genetic gift which cannot be acquired through training. Others disagree: they acknowledge that some individuals have more natural aptitude than others but maintain that the skills can be developed through insight and practice. The answer remains in dispute, largely because there has never been a systematic effort to determine what is and is not possible.

An interesting question therefore arises: even though the characteristics of artistic teaching are subtle and elusive, not easily dissected and defined, can they nevertheless be cultivated? That is, can an intuitive "feel" for what is right and wrong in teaching be developed? Parallels do exist in other forms of human endeavor. Great cooks, for example, "season to taste." They rely principally on finely honed palates which have been acquired through many years of practice. Still, students of cuisine who aspire to excellence are somehow guided toward this sense of taste from apprenticeship with a master chef. Similarly, we speak of the "nose" developed by a wine connoisseur, the "ear" of a fine musician, the "eye" of a skillful artist, and the "hand" of a great sculptor. Can we, then, make it possible for teachers to master the delicate and subtle nuances of their craft?

Little in the research literature on teacher training seems to be of any real help. Considerable work on student motivation has been done; several studies on the performance aspects of teaching can be found; and a vast body of writing on teacher professional development is available, but, somehow, none of these provides the right mix. Moreover, the technical descriptions of teaching methods in the research are themselves ambiguous and inconclusive.

The principles of learning theory are exceedingly useful, but they are not easily applied. Because of the requirements for careful control, scholarly investigation occurs in a relatively isolated and sometimes artificial setting. Teachers and students, in contrast, interact in an environment that is fraught with variables. Successful teachers are successful not so much because they follow prescribed rules as because they adapt themselves effectively to a variety of situations.

Thus, despite the vast amount of research on teaching, relatively few generalizations hold up. It has been said, in fact, that no more than twenty percent of a student's achievement is directly attributable to the teacher's efforts. This does not mean, obviously, that teachers are inconsequential. It suggests, rather, that while teachers can facilitate the process, often to a considerable degree, it is the student who does the learning.[1]

It is difficult to exaggerate the importance of incentive in learning. The capacity to grasp an idea is not dependent upon quickness alone. Some slow-learning children can only grasp a limited amount; others, however, impelled by sufficient desire, may learn as much, but at a reduced rate. In these instances, diligence and effort often counterbalance natural quickness.

The issues surrounding ability are equally nebulous. The youngsters we call bright tend to learn more quickly than those we label dull. Yet, speed in learning is not the same as depth in learning. Great intellectual insight, of course, is rarely associated with dullards. One can logically speculate that Darwin and Newton must have had brilliant minds. But the business of the school, generally speaking, is not to create Darwins and Newtons; rather it is to ensure that all children learn what they must know to live useful, productive, and satisfying lives.

"I'd caution you about taking calculus," the counselor said gently.
"Why?" the student asked, a tinge of anger in his tone.
The counselor glanced at the folder lying on the desk.
"Well, you got a C in history, an F in French, and you've had three Ds in English."
"But I got a B in chemistry," the boy said defensively. "And," he added, "I'm getting an A in physics."
The counselor looked thoughtful. "That's hard to believe," she observed.
"Ask the teacher."
The woman studied the record again silently. "Why do you do well in science, but poorly everywhere else?" she asked.
"I don't know."
"Grammar is no harder to understand than chemical valences."
"I hate grammar."
"But you like science?" the counselor questioned.
"Yes."
"Could you have done A work in English?"
"I don't know. I guess so."
The counselor glanced at the student's folder once more. "Are you smart in science?"
"No."
"How do you know?"
"Some of the other guys get it a lot faster than I do."
"How were you able to get a B in chemistry?"
"I liked it, I guess." The student hesitated. "I messed around with some of the ideas at home."
The counselor smiled. "Okay," she said, "let's schedule you for calculus."

The counselor—with perceptive insight—concluded that low achievement in one subject did not necessarily imply limited success in another. As every experienced teacher can testify, learners do best at the things that interest them.

An old aphorism holds that success and failure are both addictive. Nowhere, perhaps, is this more true than in schooling. The child who learns effectively under the ministrations of an expert teacher begins to develop a sense of adequacy and a taste for achievement. Conversely, the student who falters for one reason or another grows accustomed to faltering. Sensitive to this, gifted teachers seek to turn the psychological tides in their own favor by exploiting the natural bond between interest and achievement. Those teachers who are unable to do this eventually settle for mediocrity in their students and themselves.

Motivation (the desire to learn), *involvement* (an active interest in what is being taught), and *concentration* (sustained focus on the task) are of great significance in the classroom. Aside from their command of subject and method, great teachers excel at encouraging these qualities in their students. They weave their spell, catching their students up in the excitement of what is going on; and understanding progresses rapidly. The mechanisms they use to create willing learners, however, vary according to personal style. But more often than not, they are related to the attention-capturing principles widely used in theater: timing, surprise, suspense, emphasis of a special idiosyncrasy, and so on.

Artist teachers are not only sensitive to the importance of stimulation, they also recognize that each child responds to different incentives, has a particular reason for learning, and goes about it in an individual manner. The human ability to grasp new ideas and to learn in an infinite variety of ways is truly remarkable. It is not uncommon, standing at a bank counter where people calculate their deposits and withdrawals, to see a number of arithmetic systems in use. Each person learned a particular system of computation which, although different from other ways, is equally functional. Learning theorists generally agree that, among the standard collection of acceptable methods, one seems to work about as well as another. The odds are good, moreover, that a good teaching device for one instructor may not be the optimum choice for another. Regrettably, we cannot predict with any accuracy what teaching procedure will be most effective with a given learner, since children learn in their own special ways and at their own pace. The peculiarities of this process are difficult to fathom and often impossible to predict.

Artist teachers not only have an obvious love for their subject matter, they also take satisfaction in arousing a similar passion in their students. Yet, in their training, sadly, they are not forewarned that some aspects of the teaching art can only be acquired through experience resulting from trial and error. It might be observed, in this connection, that whereas both familiarity with basic instructional tactics and technical knowledge of a subject can be cultivated, to an extent, prior to actual teaching experience, the theater-like manipulation of student attention can only be learned in the field since it is almost totally dependent upon sensing what is needed and when.

Many, I suppose, will take these remarks as frail sentimentality, or outright foolishness. But we are in a time when large numbers of teachers are increasingly alienated, often wishing they had chosen some other career. Worse, many of those with the greatest talent for artistic teaching are leaving the profession. One of the major causes of the defection is that their teaching was not satisfying. Reduced to policies and prescriptions, constrained by rules and regulations, diminished by one temporal fad after another, teaching no longer afforded them the opportunity for self-expression.

Conceivably, a planned program wherein teachers attempt to invent, or fabricate, successful teaching procedures may be the most effective way of perpetuating individual artistry. Such a program of invention and fabrication could also yield a number of secondary benefits: The search for an effective tool might add considerable interest to a teacher's daily endeavor, give instruction a greater vitality, and heighten pride in professional craftsmanship.

The venture described in the pages which follow was based on the belief that artistry in teaching is acquirable. By studying the personal attributes of gifted teachers—their self-image and purpose, their attitudes and special sensitivities, their tendencies toward freedom and constraint, their use of dramatic flair, their ways of working—clues to professional self-development could be established.

The agenda involved identifying and observing gifted teachers; forming conclusions about the nature of artistic teaching; choosing four themes from the principles of drama; and testing—in a lengthy experiment—the idea that teachers can develop artistic qualities which enhance and enliven their teaching.

Part 1 describes the characteristics most closely associated with artistic teaching—not as imperatives in teaching, but in an effort to portray the artist teacher and to define the balance between method and style.

Part 2 provides an account of the experiment designed to test this assumption. It sketches, as well, a modest attempt to explore the theatrical dimensions of teaching.

PART ONE

Teaching As Art

When you cannot measure it, when you cannot express it in numbers, your knowledge is of a meagre and unsatisfactory kind.
                                                                                    Lord Kelvin

When you can measure it, when you can express it in numbers, your knowledge is still of a meagre and unsatisfying kind.
                                                                                    Jacob Viner

1

THE ARTIST TEACHER

Conjecturing about the mysteries of artistry is, in a sense, contrary to reason. Amorphous by nature, occurring in an infinite variety of forms, it is as difficult to analyze as to define. Yet, without some attempt to understand the infrastructure of excellence, we cannot perpetuate its development.

All artists, whatever their art, have the ability to conceive and execute tasks with exceptional taste, judgment, and imagination. Artist teachers, consequently, differ from ordinary teachers in that they function with consummate skill. Some, blessed with natural gifts, rely principally on instinct. Others, less intuitive, cultivate equally impressive artistry through practice and effort. In so doing, they often borrow insight and confidence from the methods of those whose talent is innate.

The characteristics associated with artistry come readily to mind—skill, originality, flair, dexterity, ingenuity, virtuosity, and similar qualities which, together, engender exceptional performance. One might also argue that artistry consists of master craftsmanship through which tasks are conceived, planned, and executed with unusual imagination and brilliance. From another perspective, it could be said that artistry stems from the subtle discrimination and judgment which are the byproducts of extra-ordinary perception. Regardless of the descriptive terms used, however, artistry implies human accomplishment that is unusual in its proficiency and cleverness, and greatly superior to conventional practice.

Even from this simple analysis it is plain that artistry involves attitudes as well as intentions, knowledge, discernment, astute-ness, and uncommon competence. These, moreover, must be blended together into a cohesive force: great skill wasted on trivial objectives, virtuous intentions undertaken unimaginative-ly, or ingenious tactics executed poorly defeat artistry. Applied to teaching, artistry involves (a) the choice of educational aims that have high worth, (b) the use of imaginative and innovative ways to achieve these aims, and (c) the pursuit of their achievement with great skill and dexterity. The cultivation of excellence conse-quently requires that teachers develop a shrewd conception of educational goals, exploit their capacity for creative invention in accomplishing these goals, and continually enlarge their reper-tory of technical skills.

These three efforts, moreover, must be conjoined in a nexus—a framework—that fits the classroom setting, the temper of the students, and the demands of reality. It would be senseless, for example, to choose objectives that run counter to societal expec-tations, or to devise teaching gambits which are unsuited to the learners, or at odds with the school's aspirations. Appropriate-ness, in a word, is crucial.

The best of teaching makes use of tested methods, but it is flex-ible rather than rigid. It works toward specified ends in system-atic fashion, but also allows room for adaptation to unexpected opportunity. Artistic teachers excel at improvisation. Having learned to invent when necessary, they act upon inspiration as it occurs. And if an idea fails, they are neither troubled nor discour-aged; they simply turn to something else. The capacity to create seems to be strengthened by use and weakened by disuse. For ex-ample, the experiments, described later, made clear that the usual teacher training program, both preservice and inservice, is often a liability. As the teachers tried to construct lesson staging, mood setting, and motivational activities, it became obvious that their imaginative faculties had been blunted. They repeatedly sought advice on "acceptable methods." When these requests were politely ignored, their apprehension over the need to invent rose sharply. Not only was the demand for originality threatening, but their natural aptitude for imagery, fantasy, and whimsy had been damaged by the prescriptive formulas ingrained during their professional preparation.

Common sense, intuition, and conceptualization appear to have become a lost cause in teacher education. The loss is perhaps understandable—in view of our strenuous efforts to devise more precise instructional programs—but it is nevertheless regrettable. Inspired teaching cannot be prefabricated. This is not to say, obviously, that research on pedagogy should cease, or that teachers should not be trained in techniques that have been found effective. There are, however, subtleties in teaching which cannot be prescribed in advance. A major dimension of artistry, in fact, involves the ability to take advantage of unanticipated opportunities— to capitalize on the ripeness of the moment. While expert teachers are, of course, organized in one fashion or another, they are nonetheless able to temper a plan, precipitate serendipity, or exploit chance situations when they occur.

The teachers who eventually attained the highest level of artistry were characterized by four primary attributes: first, they made a great many teaching decisions intuitively; second, they had a strong grasp of their subject as well as a perceptive understanding of their students; third, they were secure in their competence and expected to be successful; and fourth, they were exceedingly imaginative.

"Friday's test," the teacher said perfunctorily, "is on the Civil War." Noting a look of apprehension on several students' faces, she added: "It shouldn't be too bad. You can bone up by reviewing the main ideas in Chapter 11. And you might also find it helpful to go over your notes from Tuesday's discussion. Any questions?"
A long silence filled the room.
"What's wrong?" the teacher asked amiably.
"We have too many tests," a student finally muttered.
"Maybe so," the teacher replied, "but it's the only way to make sure everyone understands the main ideas."
"Tests are really stupid," said another student flatly.
"Why?" the teacher challenged.
A girl raised her hand. Receiving an encouraging nod from the teacher, she said quietly: "We have to spend a lot of time getting ready for the tests. But it's a waste because we forget the stuff as soon as the exam is over. Besides," she continued, "you grade on percentages so we have to compete. Competition is dumb."

The teacher glanced around the classroom thoughtfully, measuring the reaction of other students. Suddenly she smiled. "Perhaps you are tired of tests. But I have to be certain you know the material. What would you think of this?" she asked with sudden inspiration. "Instead of taking a test Friday, how about making up a test?"

"What do you mean?" a boy inquired from the back of the room.

"Well, instead of studying for the exam, each of you prepare a test. Just pretend that you are the teacher, and you want to find out whether your students have learned the main ideas."

A sudden flash of interest crossed the students' faces.

"How will you grade us?" someone asked.

"Well, I'll simply judge the quality of your test."

The room grew silent for a moment.

"How do you make out a good test?" a student asked, grinning.

"Ah!" the teacher said. "First of all, a good test is neither so easy that everyone can get all the questions right, nor so hard that everyone will miss each item. Secondly," she continued, "a good test deals with the big ideas, the really significant points, not the minor details. And the test questions must be written clearly enough that their meaning won't be misinterpreted. Finally," the teacher explained, "a good examination is reasonably easy to score. If a teacher has to spend two or three hours grading one student's work, she's probably using the wrong kind of a test."

"In other words," a student said, "you'll grade each of us on how good our test is."

"Right."

Once more there was silence.

"Well?" said the teacher.

"Let's try it," exclaimed a boy in the front.

A chorus of agreement followed.

Several aspects of the teacher's maneuvering are noteworthy. For example, she improved rapport and enhanced morale by hearing and acknowledging the students' concern. In addition, the unusual alternative she proposed not only appealed to the class but also permitted the testing—which she considered vital—to occur. Like all good teachers, she needed to know whether the objective had been accomplished, the extent to which the key ideas had been assimilated, the students who would require a bit more help, and so forth. The novel and unexpected nature of the tactic, moreover, brought an element of spontaneity to the classroom, temporarily relieving repetition and routine, the ubiquitous bane of schooling.

But the true brilliance of the stroke lay in the potency of the substitute examination. The class was captivated by the role reversal, as well as intrigued with the idea of giving, rather than taking, a test. Intuitively, perhaps, the teacher recognized that, to construct a test, the students would have to learn the material more thoroughly than would be necessary if they were to take one devised by someone else. Precisely for this reason, of course, she carefully listed the qualities of a good examination.

Such incidents are altogether too rare in education. They reflect artistry because they go beyond the usual conception of instruction. They cannot be invented according to formula, and the occasions when they are useful cannot, with any exactness, be specified in advance. They stem from an instinctive knowledge—a kind of sixth sense—that develops with experience and seasoning. But they may have more impact on the quality of classroom life than any particular instructional technique or textbook.

Imagination gives birth to the uniqueness, idiosyncrasy, and personalized style which are the wellspring of artistry. Teachers whose creative talents have not grown fallow through neglect are far more able to excite the emotions, to tempt curiosity, to infect learning with playfulness and pleasure, and to act upon artful impulse.

Every teacher has a special way of doing things, a manner or style that makes the teacher what he or she is. Style is a composite of the teacher's demeanor and conduct, apparent in the things teachers emphasize, in the procedures they use, and in their reactions to opportunity, adversity, failure, and success. It is reflected in both good teaching and bad, because each practitioner goes at his or her work differently.

Manner in teaching stems from choices among alternatives. Every instructional goal can be accomplished in a variety of ways, and the choices teachers make are the outgrowth of individual values, self-image, and conception of role. Thus manner evolves from self-discovery and experience. Eventually it crystallizes into a profile which reflects the individual teacher's personality, talents, and ideology.

Behind every human achievement there is some internal force which impels the individual and which, in turn, is nourished by the attainment. This is particularly true in pedagogy, where the margin between the best and the worst of performers is exceedingly large. Great teachers are inspired by the significance they attach to their work and by the pleasure they take in fostering intellectual growth.

Teaching styles, like life styles, can result in either self-fulfillment or self-deprivation. Gifted teachers, who find great personal satisfaction in their work, tend to view teaching not only as a job, but as a means of satisfying the demands of the spirit as well. All artists use their medium to express thought and feeling. When they are good enough, and strong enough, to maintain a fidelity to conviction, their labor becomes a personal creed. In contrast to those who wallow in joyless pedantry or who are governed by petty neuroses, artist teachers are open to new experiences and new sources of satisfaction.

Play can be work, just as work can be play. For the happiest of teachers, the classroom is both a calling and an intrinsic part of the good life. It offers a purpose for their energy. Their classroom manner, consequently, is a manifestation of the way they see themselves and the way they conceive of personal involvement and responsibility.

While teaching artistry, of course, cannot be reduced to a formula, useful clues can be extracted from the approaches used by exceptional practitioners. During the course of the experiment's several years, the characteristics of great teachers gradually became more clear. Cast in the form of practical suggestions, a list might read as follows:

1. *Focus on the subtleties of teaching—motivation, pacing, control—which invigorate basic instructional methods and subject matter.* Content and techniques alone do not determine success in teaching, but rather, it is the way in which they are used. Artist teachers are adept at sustaining incentive, anticipating fatigue, and managing work flow. Good methods, per se, do not guarantee success.

2. *Improvise tactics for reaching objectives and overcoming difficulties.* Teaching situations vary. Many impediments cannot be anticipated in advance, and the best techniques often cannot be preprogrammed. Thus, artist teachers are, of necessity, inventive: they devise contests, exercises, learning games, review devices, and assignments as the need arises. By constantly searching for alternatives, they maximize their chances to succeed.

3. *Take advantage of opportunities to clarify ideas and reinforce*

concepts. A degree of spontaneity is indispensable in teaching. Students unexpectedly become listless or excited. Moreover, from time to time, particular circumstances make it possible to emphasize a principle, or exploit momentary curiosity, or expand insight. It is essential, consequently, to capitalize upon such moments when they occur.

4. *Make use of intuition and hunch in modifying routine practices.* Children are not always predictable. Few lessons go exactly as planned. In addition, when problems arise, choices frequently must be exercised quickly. Teaching experience sharpens intuitive judgment to the point where it sometimes is more useful than prolonged deliberation.

5. *Set high expectations for yourself and your students.* High expectations offer several benefits. What we view as "acceptable performance" generally falls within a range. As a result, high aims tend to increase achievement. Second, large expectations function as a psychological spur: they stir the adrenaline, impelling greater effort. Third, increased achievement usually results in greater personal satisfaction. And, as a consequence, one's self-image leans toward excellence rather than mediocrity.

6. *Find the most efficient and expedient ways of getting things done.* Some procedures are a good deal more efficacious than others. It is amazing how often we can find better methods by simply examining various options. The quest for efficiency is almost second nature among artist teachers.

7. *Use temporary digressions on related topics to enrich lessons, stimulate interest, and increase pace.* Our preference for rapid change and complexity is the natural consequence of a high-tech age. Relevant excursions from the central theme, furthermore, help put ideas in context and highlight their utility, thereby increasing learning. Adroit additions add blossoms to the bare limbs of a lesson.

8. *Base your control of learning activities on student behavior.* Artistry is perhaps most apparent in the ways teachers work their students. In teaching, there are times when further explanations are desirable, times when mild chiding is necessary, times when the teacher should be sympathetic, and times when a short test is more appropriate than extended discussion. Artist teachers are sensitive to what is needed at a given moment, and follow their instincts more than formula.

9. *Take pride in what you do and in the achievement of your students.* The self-concept of teachers has diminished sharply in recent times. Inadequate salaries and lack of external support indicate that the public has devaluated the profession. No society can flourish without good education, and few human endeavors are more important than passing on our cultural heritage. The social contributions made by fine teachers are hard to exaggerate.

10. *Concentrate on a few dominant goals, central to your purpose.* All great teachers have a sense of mission. Although their aims vary, each is driven by special passions: cultivating self-direction, ensuring mastery of grammar, developing critical thinking skills, and so on. These goals, along with the major elements of the curriculum, command most of their attention. Artist teachers, in short, do not allow their energies—or those of their students—to be dissipated on insignificant activity.

11. *Respect your convictions.* Ideally, children should be exposed to a variety of great teaching, not one repetitive pattern. Healthy diversity and broader learning occur when teachers march to their own drum beat and follow their own beliefs. This commitment to ideal, obviously, also helps increase the individual's feeling of worth and accomplishment. For the best practitioners, teaching is a personal calling.

12. *Devote as much time as possible to whatever you enjoy most in teaching.* The benefits of enjoying one's work are obvious: the hazards of drudgery are eliminated, the agreeable replaces the disagreeable, and a sense of well-being is enhanced. The teaching-learning situation, we should remember, offers endless choices; students, for example, can be guided into doing much of their own learning. Gifted teachers, consequently, organize their teaching days to assure considerable self-satisfaction.

2

ARTISTRY AND CREATIVITY

One cannot collect a group of teachers and simply tell them to be more creative. Needing some sort of guide, the teachers involved in the project were given a brief description of the stages in the creative process. The nature of these stages varies from theorist to theorist, but most reflect the conception set forth long ago by Graham Wallas.[1] The creator progresses successively through periods of

1. preparation
2. incubation
3. illumination
4. verification

The *preparation* period includes such things as identifying a problem, collecting preliminary information, and considering alternative actions. Conscious work on the problem then begins and is continued as long as possible. During this time, the problem may be redefined, unworkable ideas discarded, and new approaches tried. A point may be reached, however, when the

individual becomes frustrated because the problem seems insolv-
able. The problem is then set aside temporarily. This backing off
initiates the period of *incubation*.

What actually transpires during incubation is uncertain, but
some researchers have conjectured that the unconscious mind
takes over and continues, in some unfathomable way, to work on
the problem. Sooner or later, however, if fate is kind, the creator—seemingly out of nowhere—suddenly and unexpectedly
perceives a new possibility. This leads to the third period, *illumination*.

Illumination is the onset of fresh insight. It is that magical moment when the individual says, ''Aha,'' and begins to focus on a
different approach. Illumination takes place in unpredictable
ways and under a variety of circumstances. It may ensue while
the person is asleep or awake, engaged in some mundane task, or
idly daydreaming. It may ensue quickly or a relatively long time
after the problem has been put aside. Illumination invariably
brings a sense of exuberance and triumph.

The final period is one of *verification*, where the solution reached
during illumination is tested to determine whether it really solves
the problem.

Such a description of the process is, to be sure, only approxi-
mate. In any given creative act, the periods may be telescoped,
one or another may be bypassed, or the cycle may be repeated
several times before the creator is satisfied.

The principal reason for explaining the creative process was to
establish a framework so that the teachers would know what to
expect. The source of the problem, or the reason for seeking a
novel solution, is not particularly important. It can be provoked
by an internal or external circumstance. A principal, for example,
may ask a teacher to develop a plan for ''mainstreaming''; or the
teacher may decide to do something about her students' lack of
interest in geography; or several teachers may collaborate in an
effort to reduce truancy. What does matter, however, is that the
problem must have significance for the individual, since a creative
solution is not likely to evolve until it becomes a challenge. For if
the dilemma is not internalized to the point where it is personally
meaningful, the necessary cognitive energy is not activated. Since
creative endeavor requires a good deal of perseverance and will,
motivation is crucial. Similarly, creative invention can only

happen after a problem has been formulated in one's own terms. For these reasons, the teachers were given complete latitude in choosing the topics within the four themes on which they wished to work.

During the preliminary orientation, I also pointed out that logical and systematic analysis can be antithetical to fresh insight. People tend to think about difficulties within the confines of their habitual mental set. As a result, they are unable to view them from different perspectives, and potential solutions therefore go unrecognized. To illustrate this, we spent an hour or two on a few simple exercises which demonstrated how virtually any teaching problem can be conceived of in different ways. For example, insufficient time for a teaching unit can also be construed as an excess of content, and student disinterest can be interpreted as fatigue or irrelevance of subject matter.

Although our understanding of human creativity is far from complete, many aspects of classroom instruction can be used to expand the teacher's inventiveness. There are several benefits to such an approach. First, the use of one's creative imagination is usually satisfying. Second, because there is a direct relationship between creativity, problem solving, and learning, teaching which stimulates students' creative abilities is also likely to enhance the students' general education and the teacher's involvement with the subject. Third, creative problem solving is a transferable intellectual skill—one that can be used repeatedly in many out-of-school situations. Fourth, the cognitive analysis essential to finding creative solutions also serves to strengthen the skills of logical reasoning.

It also occurred to me that efforts to stimulate the creativity of teachers—as a step toward greater artistry—might achieve a double purpose: if teacher inventiveness could be extended, and if the teachers found the experience rewarding, there was a very good chance that they might, in turn, make parallel efforts to increase the imaginal abilities of their own students. One of the early group sessions was therefore devoted to a discussion of creative behavior—the mechanisms through which teachers can function as models for their students—and to devices for stimulating student creativity.

It is important for the teacher to remember, however, that the development of creativity should be a fringe benefit, rather than the primary mission of instruction. Two dangers, in fact, exist. The first is that stimulating creativity will interfere with the accomplishment of the lesson objectives proper. Children can learn about their local government through creative activities, but increased creativity does not replace the need to understand how the city council functions. The second danger is that stupidities will be perpetrated because the nature of creative exercise is misunderstood or misconceived, either by the student or by the teacher. Hence, student assignments designed to increase originality and independent thought must be applied judiciously; precautions must be taken to ensure that laxity and disorganization are not confused with "creative experiences."

In addition, while the creative efforts of learners probably should be evaluated somewhat differently from other classroom work, total permissiveness, aimless activity, and the elimination of all controls should be avoided. Similarly, the teacher should guard against an exaggerated student preoccupation with the exotic and a mindless obsession with being different. Moreover, there are instructional situations where inventive behavior is entirely inappropriate, since many learning objectives call for drill, memorization, and other conventional procedures. Thus, although creativity does not always occur in a systematic fashion, classroom activities for stretching a child's creative muscles can be organized systematically.

Although there is some agreement as to the characteristics of creative people—inner direction, independence in thought and action, perceptiveness, high energy, preference for novel pursuits, openness of attitude, self-sufficiency, and the ability to view the familiar in unfamiliar ways—there is a good deal less agreement as to what produces these characteristics. Therefore, in solving classroom problems, teachers often must work from tentative clues, and be guided by instinct and intuition more than by theory. We cannot, for example, produce highly creative teachers at will—we can only encourage creative behavior.

The teacher training process should, at times, permit teachers to wrestle with some unsolved problem relevant to the subject being studied. The problem should be intriguing enough to provoke interest and complex enough to be a challenge. Furthermore, the solution should evoke genuine pride. The exercise should be set up so that the evaluation of the solution is non-threatening, anxiety is minimized, a mandatory sequence of steps is not imposed, penalties are not attached to either risk-taking or failure, and unnecessary constraints are absent.

In devising such assignments, teachers should be helped to distinguish, in J.P. Guilford's terms, between convergent thinking, divergent thinking, and appraisal.[2] *Convergent thinking* refers to thought which leads one to the best, most acceptable, or most conventional answer. For example, convergent thinking is used in solving a problem such as: 30 is what percent of 150? *Divergent thinking*, in contrast, refers to thinking which takes an unusual direction and which is inspired by a search for alternatives. For example: could a new kind of can opener be designed which would be clearly superior to those now in use? *Appraisal* has to do with the way in which the adequacy, suitability, and quality of solutions to problems are judged.

Because divergent thinking and convergent thinking have different purposes, they must be appraised in different ways. In convergent thinking, the teacher frequently wants to reach a particular solution, known in advance, through a specific pattern of reasoning. In divergent thinking, no particular solution is expected and the teacher is free to pursue whatever ideas seem fruitful. The appraisal criteria, in contrast, are predominantly qualitative.

The typical curriculum is based upon verbal learning and the systematic accumulation of factual knowledge. Teachers are taught to use appropriate methods to solve problems through conventional reasoning and to discard or ignore whatever is not standard procedure. Such instruction is useful and necessary. However, originality requires that the creator look beyond the obvious, tolerate temporary ambiguity, toy with seemingly illogical alternatives, and leap intuitively, whenever possible, to an unsuspected solution. Thus the teacher benefits from an occasional opportunity to grapple with problems in a nonprescriptive manner, to speculate about notions which may, on the surface, seem irrational, and to conjecture about the unexplored potential of an idea.

Periodic practice in creative thinking may enhance the teacher's ability to pursue additional instructional objectives. A history teacher, for example, might select some historical crisis, provide the students with information on the events that caused the crisis, and ask them to "guess" how it was resolved. Their predictions could then be compared with a careful study of what actually occurred. Similarly, a chemistry teacher could give her class the scientific evidence from which a relatively obscure but reasonably simple law or principle was derived, ask the students to infer as much as they can, and then guide them through the reasoning that led to the conclusion. Asking English students to rewrite the closing sequence of a story or a play, altering the outcome in some plausible way, or requiring geometry students to invent a proof, are further examples of techniques that simultaneously teach subject matter and develop creative thinking. Creative teaching, in sum, can stimulate student creativity.

Several cautions, however, about the classroom cultivation of students' inventive capacities should be noted. First, courage in attempting an intuitive solution must be regarded as more important than finding a correct answer; a deliberate effort must be made to increase the learner's willingness to risk mistakes and to tolerate failure. Second, the evaluation of a creative idea must, therefore, be free from reward or punishment: fear of a poor grade is just as inhibitive as fear of failure. Third, the child's idea, consequently, should be judged only by its merits, by its imaginativeness rather than its propriety. Fourth, poor solutions, however, ought not to pass without comment; some sort of objective appraisal—in a benign spirit—should take place. Finally, as noted earlier, exercises in creative thought must not be used as a substitute for other instructional goals.

While opinions differ as to what is trivial and significant in education, few would deny that a mastery of basic skills and a command of fundamental information are essential. Many would also agree, however, that these alone are not enough. Ultimately, schooling must also enable students to make reasoned judgments, to exploit the powers of their intellects, and to become self-directive in acquiring new knowledge. It is at this axis that virtually all conceptions of the educational process converge: knowledge and reflective thought are critical, not only to a productive and fulfilling life, but to an enlightened citizenry as well. It follows, therefore, that both should have a place in the curriculum.

The recent renewal of interest in values education, the increased emphasis on competency-oriented teaching, the continuing belief that instruction should be as concerned with method as with content, the long-standing assumption that education should teach one how to acquire, interpret, and use knowledge, and the growing awareness that intelligence quotients, achievement scores, grades, and college degrees have little real bearing on a satisfying adulthood—all suggest that we are remiss when we conceive of the school solely as a dispenser of stock information. The discovery of an ability may, in the long run, be worth more to the student than the assimilation of factual lore. One of the distinctions between wisdom and knowledge, after all, is that only the latter is subject to obsolescence.

The basics are, of course, vital. Without them there is nothing upon which to build. But a complete education consists of something more than the basics. If we are to achieve our mission we must nurture talent as well as knowledge. Creativity—so common in the behavior of the first grader and so rare in that of the graduate student—does not have to be wasted by lifeless classrooms.

Assuming that creativity is important not only in teacher training but in teaching itself, I stressed in the experimental program three basic kinds of creativity. Some creativity, for example, stems from the creator's aesthetic impulse. A painting, poem, symphony, sculpture, or classroom display is the outgrowth of such self-expression.

Another kind of creativity is problem-oriented. That is, the creator constructs a problem and seeks an answer. Scientists involved in cancer research engage in this sort of creativity. Similarly, economists who speculate about the control of inflation, automotive engineers who try to build a faster racing car, and enterprising teachers who search for a way to help a youngster grasp the principle of cultural diffusion all exhibit problem-solving creativity.

The third kind of creativity is essentially a combination of the first two. The creator attempts to find a solution to a problem, but the solution is, at the same time, a form of personal expression. An architect, for instance, may design a building to fit a client's requirements, thus solving a problem, but the building is also a reflection of the architect's artistic values and personal commitment. Creativity in teaching is of this third variety: teachers use their imagination and inventiveness to facilitate learning, but their contrivances are related to their educational ideology, their sense of role, their convictions regarding good and bad teaching, and their beliefs about the things children need. As a result, a creative teaching strategy is not only a manifestation of artistry, but personally symbolic and intrinsically rewarding as well.

"Respect your convictions," artist teachers counsel. Teaching excellence stems, not just from exceptional skill, but also from a personal creed about what teaching is and should do. Every artist teacher has a set of beliefs about what makes for good or bad teaching and learning. These beliefs are self-determined, molded over time, and establish the infrastructure of the teacher's classroom approach. Coupled with style, they give the teaching individuality and character. Exposure to different teaching, reflecting differing convictions, makes the overall educational experience a better one for students.

Respecting private beliefs, moreover, is essential to a teacher's psychological well-being. Work becomes purposeful, pleasure in labor increases, and creative energies can be directed at matters of importance. Conversely, ignoring these convictions results in psychological damage and reduced effectiveness.

In order to synthesize our discussion of creativity and to provide a working guide, the teachers in the program were given a copy of six simple postulates:

1. Creativity is not restricted to specially gifted individuals but exists, to a greater or lesser degree, in everyone.
2. The creative potential of teachers can be developed and expanded through deliberate effort.
3. Creative teaching is valuable, first, because it enhances artistry; and second, because it also tends to stimulate creative behavior in students.
4. One can approach teaching in ways that utilize creative artistry, or in ways that inhibit it.
5. Creativity in teaching not only makes instruction less monotonous and wearisome but, under proper controls, far more potent.
6. Teaching devoid of creativity is, at best, routine; and, at worst, ineffectual.

These postulates were often made a part of the experimental

activities. The purpose was to implant a state of mind. Possibly, if an attitude that increased creativity in teaching could be instilled, there would be permanent benefits for both students and teachers. But if the participants were merely exposed to a repertory of convenient gimmicks, the gains would be far more temporal. Hence the teachers were urged to approach not only the four themes, but all of their teaching, as a creative problem—to internalize a creative attitude that would stay with them and that could be passed on to their students.

Teachers who have a genuine investment in their calling—who think the work they do is important—often invent maneuvers to perpetuate learning they regard as particularly crucial. A teacher in Texas, for example, is inordinately proud of the fact that, over a twenty-year span, every student she has taught English has learned to diagram sentences. A few years back, a slow student having unusual difficulty was hired by the teacher to mow her lawn on Saturday afternoons. Midway in the mowing, the student was required to come in the house, sip lemonade, and receive a special tutoring in the mechanics of sentence structure.

A teacher in Canada with a passion for effective vocabulary developed a game where students had to eliminate one word in a sentence and substitute two others. "The child yelled," for example, would be changed to, "The child screamed furiously." The next student would then delete "child" and change the sentence to, "The angry infant screamed furiously." After another student's revision the sentence became, "The wildly infuriated infant screamed furiously." For teachers who really care about children learning, inventiveness is personally symbolic of their professional values.

In teaching, creativity and artistry are inseparable. Truly great teachers not only have an instinctive sense about how to work with children, as well as a talent for distinguishing between the significant and the trivial, but they also are able to approach their tasks with fresh vision. Once they have decided upon their objectives, they seek the approach that offers optimum advantage. At this point their creative impulses begin to take hold: they shun the tedious, the mundane, the prosaic, and look for methods which are novel and appealing. In addition, since no teaching strategy is foolproof, and difficulties can arise in even the most skillfully planned lesson, the creative aspects of artistry are also important in localizing the sources of difficulties and devising shrewd remedies. It is not student failure, but the ability to overcome student failure, that separates strong teaching from weak.[3]

Inventiveness, consequently, is virtually essential to effective teaching. In its simpler forms, inventiveness involves adapting lessons to the needs of each class. In its more complex states, it consists of devising ways to solve instructional problems. Artist teachers routinely *improvise tactics for reaching objectives and overcoming difficulties*. Improvisation is important because modifications and adjustments are almost always necessary to improve student learning rate and achievement. Classrooms differ considerably, and conventional practices do not always work. Learning, moreover, sometimes involves special factors which must be taken into account. The best solutions, therefore, are the result of deliberate efforts to accommodate circumstances by manipulating one thing or another.

> *After three separate efforts to teach the principle of exposition, development, and recapitulation in music—each of which failed—the teacher was at wit's end. Having repeatedly reminded her students that composers like Wagner depended on the listeners remembering earlier themes, so as to recognize their later elaboration, she was determined to make her students understand musical form, no matter what it took.*
>
> *The class had little trouble with simple variations and could easily identify themes which were repeated in a related key, but when it came to the development sections, the students' attention focused on the new detail to such an extent that they no longer "heard" the basic motif. For a week or two, the young teacher fretted over the problem. She discarded one idea after another as either too complicated or impractical. Older teachers advised her to go on with something else, suggesting that she was overly ambitious, and that such discrimination was impossible without formal music training. Still, the teacher searched in her mind for a solution.*
>
> *One afternoon, during the lunch hour, she noticed a group of students clustered in a corner of the yard. Several girls were swaying their bodies in a rhythmic cadence. Curious, she drew closer and found that the students were listening to a new rock hit. A slender boy in the center of the group held a tape recorder in his hand. A few moments later, as the teacher continued on her noon duty rounds, a sudden inspiration took hold.*

The following day, when her music appreciation class arrived, she asked how many students had tape recorders. A dozen or so students immediately said, "I do." The teacher looked at her students pensively. "I had an idea," she said with sudden animation. "Maybe machines have better memories than people. What would you think," she added, "about trying an experiment? We could play Beethoven's 'Eroica' again, and one of you can record the theme of the second movement, when it's first introduced. Then, later, when Beethoven gets into the development section, someone else can record that segment. Finally, when he comes to the recapitulation—the restatement—we'll have a third person record again. Of course," she added, "technically, it won't be a real recapitulation because we'll select passages in the same key. If," she finished triumphantly, "we can synchronize the timing, and start all three recorders at exactly the same instant, we'll play the three recordings together and see if they fit. What do you think?"

Her students looked at her with surprise. Suddenly, however, delight appeared on their faces.

"Neat," one boy exclaimed.

"We'll have to get three recorders with the same speed," another exclaimed. "I'll bring a timer."

And so it was arranged. They had difficulty starting the recorders simultaneously; there were slight variations in their pitch; and the tempo of the recorded passages was a bit uneven; but the sounds blended sufficiently for the students to recognize their commonality.

RECAPITULATION

Ready-made solutions are not available for all classroom problems. Even when a customary method exists, circumstantial factors make each situation unique. Thus, a tailor-made procedure may bring better results. Even more importantly, it is likely that the best teaching techniques have yet to be invented. Hence, a creative experiment or two could yield new approaches superior to anything now known.

Artist teachers are self-directed. They obey an inner instinct which makes them independent and autonomous. Ever open to new possibilities, they constantly look for a better way—for an unsuspected bonanza or a novel solution to a difficulty. They like to invent, first, because invention creates alternatives, and second, because it makes teaching far more interesting.

SOME ISSUES

1. Since creation involves a risk of failure, it sometimes generates anxiety. Can teachers acquire the psychological study safety essential to inventive behavior?
2. Can teachers learn to view the familiar in unfamiliar ways, to see possibilities in the seemingly impossible? In short, can the creative spirit be cultivated?
3. Teaching must strike a judicious balance between tested formula and innovation—between adaptation and the tried and true. When should teachers follow customary routine and when should they explore different routes?

3

∽

ARTISTRY AND ATTITUDE

The ties between artistry and attitude became a topic of interest as a result of an odd set of circumstances. I had been asked to speak in one of Pennsylvania's high school districts, on the topic of teachers' attitudes. I prepared a brief overview of the standard theory on attitude development.

I pointed out that beliefs place the world where it is; they clarify objects, ideas, and thought. Values, on the other hand, give beliefs weight and direction. A value is a sort of super-belief, organizing those of lesser consequence. What we call "feeling" is really a part of believing and knowing. Feeling expresses itself in attitudes, and attitudes are values acted out, or made behavioral, at a specific time in a specific situation.

The typical format for an Institute Day talk of this sort calls for a bit of humor, some intellectual substance without excessive detail, and a closing benediction carrying words of encouragement and support. I more or less followed this agenda in my presentation. A synthesis of my remarks would have read as follows:

TEACHERS' ATTITUDES

The teacher's professional behavior springs from a deep and largely unacknowledged foundation. All people define themselves and their surroundings according to their attitudes, beliefs, and values; these impart form and meaning, both cultural and personal, to the scope of human activities. Teachers are no exception to this condition.

Because one "believes" that what one *thinks* to be true *is* true, beliefs influence the individual, whether they are based upon real or vicarious experiences. A teacher having difficulty with classroom discipline, for example, may *believe* that threat and punishment are the best ways to maintain control. The control measures resulting from this belief, however, can be counterproductive since many nonpunitive teachers have well-behaved classes. Similarly, a wealth of knowledge is of little use if the teacher feels the students are unable to learn, just as pedagogical brilliance and high scholarship are both dissipated when the teacher's attitudes are misplaced. All three factors—knowledge, skill, and belief—are of a piece and each is indispensable to good teaching.

Because of our beliefs we are inclined to react in certain ways toward an object or a situation. Instructors who both know their subjects and have a good collection of professional skills can still be weakened by erroneous beliefs. For when false conceptions are coupled with effective techniques a double tragedy occurs: the teacher works toward mistaken ends with consummate efficiency. Teachers who "believe" in quiet rooms chastise their students when the noise level seems excessive. Similarly, a principal who regards teachers as subordinates will demand greater deference than one who views them as colleagues. There are, of course, exceptions, but in general we tend to follow the habitual attitude patterns that correlate with our beliefs.

Beliefs and attitudes are essential because they make meaning out of what otherwise would be a muddle of disordered notions. They synthesize previous experiences, systematizing meaning so that, faced with a new situation, we have some inkling of what to do.

Attitudes are powerful because they predispose us to behave in particular ways. We rarely respond to situations haphazardly. Rather, we react according to the beliefs we have carefully constructed for ourselves. Most of us, in fact, have a compelling urge to honor our own convictions. Many teachers, for example, try to discourage their students from cheating on tests. They do so, not because they *know* there are dishonest students in the class, but rather because they *believe* that students will cheat if they can. To cite another example, some teachers may have the attitude that handicapped children cannot learn as effectively as normal ones. As a consequence, they lower their expectations and then fail to build the students' intellectual apparatus sufficiently. The snag, of course, is that our attitudes are often reinforced by experiences which, though real, trick us into overgeneralization. Most teachers have occasionally encountered students who cheat, and some handicapped children do have learning impairments. This does not mean, obviously, that all children are dishonest, or that every handicapped child has limited ability.

Attitudes can also lead us astray because what has been true in our past experience may not be true at present; the world may have changed more rapidly than our views, leaving us with outdated beliefs and obsolete habits. Consider, for example, the teacher who shuns computers in the classroom, convinced that books are mandatory. His convictions may reflect the beliefs of other teachers, whose opinions he shares and admires, or his own experiences. These experiences, however, may have occurred during his own schooling, or very early in his career, and may no longer provide an appropriate basis for judgment. Beliefs and attitudes, in sum, have a long history of their own, and they do not always keep up with the times.

It is easy to see from all this that attitudes—because they are the primary determinants of behavior—are crucial. Three points, in this regard, are especially significant: (1) teachers' attitudes are relatively enduring and not easily altered; (2) attitudes regarding teaching and learning are influenced by a broad array of beliefs, many of which may be irrational; (3) attitudes, in the main, govern teachers' expectations. They are likely not only to regulate classroom aims and intentions, but to affect teacher motivation as well. Attitudes are a kind of barometer of commitment. They determine what is stressed, what is slighted, and what is ignored.

The teacher who believes that children should learn to reason inductively emphasizes heuristics and invests substantial teaching energy in activities which involve problem-solving. Similarly, teachers who believe that self-discipline is important spend considerable time on control; those who prize spontaneity seek opportunities to stimulate their classes; and those who are test-conscious give frequent quizzes. It is precisely this difference in attitude, moreover, that causes one teacher to be concerned about the emotional well-being of his students while another worries only about their factual stockpile.

The place, perhaps, where teachers' attitudes have their most telling effect is in performance standards. "*Set high expectations for yourself and your students,*" the artist teachers who were interviewed during the experiment said. Pointing high has several advantages. First, it is likely to raise achievement levels. Second, improved achievement seems to alter self-concept: when we consistently produce superior results we begin to think of ourselves as superior achievers. And third, once this happens we begin to do whatever is necessary to ensure excellence. High expectations, in short, become a self-fulfilling prophecy for both teacher and student.

Several weeks after my Pennsylvania talk, I received a call from an English supervisor who attended the session. She wondered if I would clarify the common ground between attitudes, beliefs, and values. The district, she added, was preparing a teachers' guide on the teaching of values, and there was confusion as to whether to use an affective approach, involving the emotions, or a cognitive one, based upon logic and reason.

I said what I could, pointing out that it was not an either-or matter. I offered to return, at my own expense, and work with the supervisors for another half-day. She was gracious enough to demur, but as we talked on, I chanced to mention the artistry experiments. Soon we reached an agreement: I would visit the district again, invite participation in the artistry project, and at the same time, give an additional presentation on attitudes.

The gist of the second talk was as follows:

TEACHERS' ATTITUDES, VALUES, BELIEFS

Where do our attitudes come from? Psychologists have long explored this question, hoping to uncover the connective tissue between belief and behavior. Despite much useful work, we still have but a half understanding of the intricacies of attitude development. Amidst all that is yet unclear, however, a few things seem sure: attitudes are affected by multiple influences, and their relative impact fluctuates from individual to individual. There are, for example, physiological factors such as age which produce differences; the attitudes of young and old are likely to vary. Personality, too, is significant: some people are bothered by crowds while others are not. One teacher prefers friendly relationships with his students and another finds it necessary to maintain distance.

The emotions, too, have a place in the anatomy of attitudes. A person with a strong yearning for affection does not behave in the same way as one who is psychologically more self-sufficient. Some teachers, for instance, occasionally bring their classes cookies or other special treats. Gestures of this sort may be impelled more by personal need than by pedagogical convictions. The popularity that is important to one teacher may be inconsequential to another.

Beyond personality and emotion, there are faculty pressures. The wish to be accepted by coworkers exerts considerable power over attitudes. In a school where most of the faculty believe in strict regimentation, for instance, it is dangerous for one teacher to be far more tolerant and permissive than his/her colleagues. Group sanctions operate much as they do elsewhere.

For the most part, however, people's attitudes are influenced by the experiences they have accumulated, and by the significant life events etched in their psyches. A teacher who, by chance, has worked with three principals, each of whom was domineering, may develop an understandable dislike of administrators. One who has been faced with frequent discipline problems may be likely to avoid classroom activities that give children considerable freedom. And, in the same spirit, a teacher who once experienced acute embarrassment during a student discussion of human reproduction may oppose sex education, just as one who has endured the hostility of irate parents will go to great lengths to guard against community criticism.

Are beliefs, attitudes, and values interdependent? Beliefs, like the attitudes they breed, serve two important functions: (1) they define the effect of the universe on the self, and (2) they define the self in relation to others. Some beliefs are rooted in existential

ideas formed early in childhood. Others are closely allied with the
gratification of desires. Still others are created by shifts in our
cognitive structure which develop when new experiences require
that old conceptions be modified.

Values are beliefs which deal with appropriate goals and
behavior. They separate convictions about matters of high importance (primary beliefs) from those of less consequence (secondary
beliefs). We may believe, for example, that oranges are more
nutritional than apples, that swimming is more fun than walking,
and that cheating on income taxes is immoral. These beliefs,
however, are not of the same significance: cheating on a tax
return probably would bother most of us more than eating an
orange or substituting a walk for a swim.

Because they serve as the connection between objects and concepts, values prejudice the cognitive process. They are not attained
by thinking through: rather, the raw material of thought—our sensory data—is sorted out by our values. Thus, emotion and reason
are interacting phenomena. Susanne Langer argued, for instance,
that cognition should be subsumed under feeling. ''Value exists
only where there is consciousness. Where nothing is felt, nothing
matters.''[1] Values convert feelings into a cognitive network.

As a result, our interpretation of truth is conditioned by our
beliefs, attitudes, and values. What *should be* true is never completely separated from what *is* true, and, as a result, our notions
of truth and falsity (that is, what we *believe* to be true or false)
sometimes clash with reality. The stronger our values, the more likely it is that concepts which reinforce them will be regarded as fact.

To summarize, then, our values help us determine what we
regard as appropriate attitudes toward people and ideas. Once
formed, they define for us what we would like ourselves and our
world to be, and, to an extent, what we actually think it to be.
Although what we value is heavily affected by what we know,
the reverse is equally true: our knowledge is also influenced by
our values. Hence, the interplay between attitudes, beliefs, and
values, like that between thought and action, is interdependent.
Each affects, and is affected, by the other.

Following the second presentation we talked about the topic
for a half-hour or so, and then went on to the second meeting,
where I described the artistry experiments. I outlined the general

nature of the project and asked for questions. An exceedingly articulate man, who I later learned was an elementary school principal, wished to know whether the artistry activities would improve teachers' attitudes. A bit surprised, I countered with a question of my own: why was he concerned about teachers' attitudes? In the ensuing discussion, I discovered that the district—worried about "burn-out"—had previously tried, with little success, to organize an inservice program that would bring about a more positive attitude among teachers.

While the dialogue was interesting, it did not seem to get anywhere. I was obliged to acknowledge that I had as yet no idea whether the artistry activities would affect teachers' attitudes or not. I volunteered to prepare a short statement on teacher attitudinal change, for consideration at a future principals' meeting, knowing that I would have to return in any event to learn the district's response to the artistry invitation.

The statement, somewhat abridged to avoid further imposition on the reader's patience, read as follows:

TEACHERS' ATTITUDES AND STAFF DEVELOPMENT

Since attitudes have a profound effect on teaching behavior, it is curious that teacher training has so often ignored them. Conversations with teachers in the artistry experiment and elsewhere would seem to suggest that there have been several other failings as well:

First, we assume that attitudes and beliefs can be changed through mandate, exhortation, or lecture. Unfortunately, human impulse is made of firmer stuff. Beliefs run too deep to be easily swayed by words, whether printed or spoken. Usually they must be modified through the same processes by which they were formed—consistent experiences accumulated over time.

Second, we seldom bother to explore the specific attitudes which are prerequisite to the effective use of a program or method. If a teacher believes, for example, that all children must use the same basic drills, staff development aimed at individualization is virtually hopeless. For the same reasons, inservice programs dealing with aesthetic experiences are likely to be useless when a teacher thinks that everything learned can be measured on a test. There must, therefore, be a reasonable fit between the teacher's attitudes and the methods advocated in teacher workshops.

Third, the time allotted to a professional development activity is usually short, whereas the time required for authentic attitudinal change is usually long. It may take more time for teachers to develop faith in a technique than to learn its use. The open classroom, for example, met with difficulties because many teachers questioned its utility.

Fourth, in teacher training we tend to be concerned almost exclusively with rational thought. Preoccupied with what we think teachers should know and be able to do, we give little attention to what they feel. Worse, we overlook their uniqueness and individuality. One teacher may be driven by a need for order and tranquillity, another by a strong desire for recognition, and a third by a fear of failure. We foolishly assume that any good inservice program will be right for any teacher in any situation.

Fifth, because attitude is an abstraction, a theoretical construct that is difficult to assess, we underestimate both its impact and complexity. To alter teachers' attitudes regarding teaching, we must deal with what they know, how they feel, and how they act. A teacher, for example, may *know* that children have aggressive tendencies, *feel* angry when such aggression occurs, and *act* in ways that either offset or express the anger. Said another way, the teaching behavior prompted by a particular attitude may be based on assumptions, knowledge, or emotional leanings.

It is also obvious that a teacher's work is influenced as much by personal attitudes as professional ones. The art teacher who believes his life has been wasted, the chemistry instructor who feels that suffering is good for the soul, and the counselor who thinks that people cannot really change are weakened professionally by their convictions. Hence emotional health—at least to a degree—is prerequisite to pedagogical health.

Take pride in what you do, and in the achievement of your students. Artist teachers have considerable self-respect. They believe what they do is valuable, and find great satisfaction in doing it well. Thus, their emotional health and pedagogical health are mutually reinforcing.

There is a great difference between the worker who performs for a wage and the one who thinks his or her efforts are of benefit to society. Of late, the missionary spirit, so characteristic of previous generations of teachers, has all but expired.

Many teachers have left the profession. Insufficient parental support, increasing problems with discipline, diminished income, and the continuing intrusion of nonteaching tasks have had their cumulative effect. Still, many artist teachers have chosen to remain in the schools. Asked why, they are likely to say, "Somehow, when that magical look of understanding comes into the kids' eyes, it's all worthwhile!" For such teachers, the rewards of teaching are to be found in the unfolding of children's minds, rather than in salary or status.

We cannot instill an interest in better instruction through admonitions. Our endless effort to do so, despite an unremitting lack of success, is a lasting tribute to our myopia. What teachers value may be of more consequence than what they know. The alienation caused by "burn-out," for example, is largely attributable to job dissatisfaction stemming from a sense of underachievement. How else is it possible to explain the person who feels inadequate despite great accomplishment or the unhappiness of the individual who seemingly has everything? As the foundation of conscious or unconscious choice, attitudes label, as Alfred North Whitehead said, "matters of importance" as opposed to matters of fact. Over the course of their careers, teachers form a number of convictions about children, learning, and instruction. Whatever the source of these convictions, they sway the individual in one direction or another. Whether based on fact or fancy, they heavily influence the teacher's approach. In view of the profound role attitudes play, it is surprising that they do not receive greater attention in teacher training.

Because attitudes, beliefs, and values are so critical in determining not only teacher motivation, but teacher effectiveness and self-satisfaction as well, it seemed important to discover what kinds of attitudes distinguish artist teachers. The research in this area is comparatively limited, but it seemed possible that teachers' subjective responses to typical classroom situations might provide some hints and suggest new areas of exploration. To test this possibility, I developed a number of multiple-choice items with which to compare attitudes. Several of these are reproduced, for purposes of illustration, here:

For some inexplicable reason, a seventh-grade math class became bored with the assignment. A few students began to whisper; several stared idly into space; and two boys got into an argument over an eraser. The teacher did nothing. He should have:

a. called the class to order by threatening punishment.
b. warned the students who were not working that they would have to complete the assignment as homework.
c. wandered about the room, monitoring the students more closely.
d. ended the lesson and shifted to a different activity.

In working with children of limited ability:

a. there is only so much a teacher can do.
b. repeated encouragement will improve achievement.
c. excessive prodding may increase anxiety.
d. skillful teaching can sometimes overcome learning difficulties.

Teachers periodically encounter sections in textbooks which seem too difficult for the class. In such situations it is best to:

a. skip the section.
b. substitute a simplified version of the material.
c. teach the section as it is.
d. use special techniques to make the material more understandable.

Once the multiple-choice items were available, I identified a number of teachers who—on the strength of their creative inventions—seemed exceptionally able. To confirm my judgment, I also conferred with the teachers' principals, eliminating those who were not highly rated. I then asked the selected group, as well as a representative sampling of other participants, to score the items. This informal procedure gave me two groups—one average and one outstanding—to compare.

The more artistic teachers tended to favor option (d) in each item. As the discerning reader may already have inferred, the (d) options all imply that in teaching where there is a will there usually is a way.

Seemingly, then, the attitudes of fine teachers do vary from those of the run-of-the-mill practitioner. Artist teachers are more flexible, more willing to experiment, and more personally involved in their students' success. They also seem to have a greater faith in their own power. Egocentricity, in teaching, may not be all bad.

It is attitude, mainly, that causes artist teachers to *focus on the subtleties of teaching—motivation, pacing, control—which invigorate basic instructional methods and subject matter.* They know that methods are only devices, and that their method of use makes considerable difference. They organize their system of control, their management procedures, their motivational lures *before* they select technique and content, since these are central to effective teaching and a necessary concomitant of every method. Because they want excellent results, they are willing to spend a good deal of time attending to the fine details which—in the last analysis—are far more important than we might think.

RECAPITULATION

Artist teachers invest more in, and profit more from, their work. In contrast to mediocre teachers, they are extremely concerned about their own and their students' success. To perpetuate good results, they experiment freely, often replacing a routine maneuver with something that is better. They aim high, go the extra step, and do whatever is necessary to accomplish their objectives. In sum, they value personal excellence and have the self-image of a winner. They enjoy their reputation as great teachers and believe that, in one way or another, excellent performance is always attainable. To achieve exceptional results, they give careful thought and attention not only to method and content but also to supporting details. In their classrooms, materials are passed out and milk money collected with as much finesse as everything else.

SOME ISSUES

1. Since teachers act out their beliefs and values, how can these be influenced?
2. Some teachers occasionally labor under misconceptions about teaching and learning process. Such attitudes are not easily changed. What experiences best correct these misconceptions?
3. Personality characteristics can be productive (the desire to excel) as well as counterproductive (a penchant for convenience). Can these characteristics be modified? If so, how?

4

⤟

ARTISTRY AND PERCEPTION

What we *believe* to be possible seems to have a bearing on what *is* possible. A bank thought to be on the verge of failure may have a run on its deposits and become bankrupt even if the original supposition was unfounded. Similarly, a boy who is told that he has little athletic ability may not compete and thus fail to develop latent talents. Our self-perceptions, though initially false, may lead us to behavior that eventually makes them true. In this context, teachers' expectations are of crucial importance in the day-to-day operation of the classroom.

Evidence to support this conclusion comes initially from animal research. Robert Rosenthal described a classic experiment:

A class in experimental psychology had been performing experiments with human subjects for most of a semester. Now they were asked to perform one more experiment, the last in the course, and the first employing animal subjects. The experimenters were told of studies that had shown that maze-dullness could be developed in strains of rats by successive inbreeding of the poorly performing maze-runners. There were sixty perfectly ordinary laboratory rats available, and they were equitably divided among the twelve experimenters. But half the experimenters were told that their rats were maze-dull. The animal's task was to learn to run to the darker of two arms of an elevated T-shaped maze.[1]

Beginning with the first day, and henceforth throughout the experiment, the animals thought by the researchers to be "brighter" performed better. Replications by other investigators have produced similar results. The attitudes of the experimenters toward the rats determined in advance how the rats would perform.

Corresponding conclusions have been reached in a number of other studies involving human behavior. James Chambliss, for example, studied two groups of boys who were involved repeatedly in delinquent activities. He named one group, consisting of middle-class boys, the "Saints," and the other group, from lower-class homes, the "Roughnecks." Classroom observers, in watching both groups, found that neither did much studying. Chambliss therefore was puzzled as to why the Saints consistently received better grades than the Roughnecks. After talking with the teachers, he concluded that:

> . . . the teachers, by their own admission, were inclined to give these boys (and presumably others like them) the "benefit of the doubt." When asked about how the boys did in school, and when pressed on specific examinations, teachers admitted that they were disappointed in x's performance, but quickly added they "knew he was capable of doing better" so the boy was given a higher grade than he had actually earned. How often this happened is impossible to know. During the two years that I observed the group, I never once saw any of the boys take homework home.[2]

Accurate perceptions in the classroom is important, first, because much of the teacher's instructional maneuvering is guided by perceptual data; second, because teachers' beliefs often make them vulnerable to perceptual distortion; and third, because perceptions heavily influence teachers' goals and expectations.

Differential perception permits one person to see an object as beautiful and another to see it as ugly. Perceptual disparities, moreover, are particularly significant in rule laden institutions like the school. People can choose their favorite ice cream, attend either an art exhibit or tennis match, and wear blue or brown;

however, relatively few individuals are sufficiently privileged to choose a preferred brand of education. Moreover, opinions differ, particularly among teachers, as to what constitutes good teaching. It is hardly surprising, therefore, that perceptual differences lead to endless criticism. Unfortunately, educational criticism is most notable for its diversity and inconsistency. Examples of conflicting perceptions abound. Many people, for example, write the editors of their newspapers, asking that discipline be tightened, instruction be made more rigorous, and "frivolities" be eliminated. Charles Reich, on the other hand, casting a baleful eye upon school, had this to say:

> School is intensely concerned with training students to stop thinking and start obeying. Any course that starts with a textbook and a teacher and ends with an examination runs this danger unless great pains are taken to show students that they are supposed to think for themselves; in most school and college classes, on the other hand, thinking for oneself is actually penalized, and the student learns the value of repeating what he is told. Public school is "obedience school"; the student is taught to accept authority without question, to respect authority simply because of its position, to obey not merely in the area of school regulations but in the area of facts and ideas as well.[3]

While many Americans are unhappy about some aspects of schooling, not all would agree with Reich's point of view. Many, ironically, fault the schools for not doing more of exactly what he opposes.

A survey by the American College Testing Programs yielded similar evidence of perceptual inconsistency.[4] The survey of high school graduates' reactions to their school experiences revealed that although some preferred an easy ride, others wanted to be worked hard. The two characteristics most frequently mentioned when students were asked to described the qualities of good teachers were "demanding" and "caring." Typical reactions were: "My best teacher was the strictest. She made us work our tails off, with papers once a week and daily quizzes, but she taught. She made us understand, which is the great thing about a good teacher."

"My very best teacher was one I hated. She sure knows how to teach English, though. I learned."

Asked to suggest improvements in high school practices, the

students advised teachers to guard against cheating, avoid excessive fraternization and permissiveness, and to be fair—but hardnosed—about regulations. "Students," they said, "still need rules even though they feel they do not."

Similarly, students' perceptions of their teachers often influence behavior. Consider the following school incident which occurred not in the busy, hectic atmosphere of the classroom, but in a one-to-one counseling session. James, a black boy of school age, had earlier been interviewed by a clinician and was awaiting a second interview. He had been described, in the initial report, as "sullen, surly, slow, unresponsive, apathetic, unimaginative, and lacking inner life."

> James was seated in an adjoining room waiting to go into the clinician's office. It was just after the lunch hour and James had the first afternoon appointment. The conclusion of the lunch break on this particular day was used by the staff to present a surprise birthday cake to one of the clinicians who happened to be a Negro. The beautifully decorated cake was brought in and handed to the recipient by James' clinician who was white, as were all the other members of the staff. The Negro woman was deeply moved by the cake—and the entire surprise. In a moment of great feeling, she warmly embraced the giver of the cake. James inadvertently perceived all this from his vantage point in the outer office. That afternoon he showed amazing alacrity in taking the tests and responding in the interview. He was no longer sullen and dull. On the contrary, he seemed alive, enthusiastic, and he answered questions readily. His psychologist was astonished at the change and in the course of the next few weeks retested James on the test on which he had done so poorly. He now showed marked improvement and she quickly revised not only the test appraisal of him on the clinical record card, but her general personality description of him as well.[5]

Admittedly, the situations described here are largely circumstantial. There is, nonetheless, abundant evidence that the quality of learning is at least partly attributable to the way students perceive teachers' behavior and the way students are seen and treated by their teachers. The child who assumes that his teacher's actions are the result of his own incompetence soon begins to feel incompetent. Thus teacher misperceptions that lead to a lack of faith in their students' abilities, or to erroneous expectations, have serious consequences.

Our views of people and events, as we saw earlier, are conditioned by beliefs, attitudes, and values. The aims of teachers and students alike, both influence, and are influenced by, their perceptions. Thus perceptual errors often result in human actions which have been prompted either by a false sense of reality or a distortion of reality. It is because perception involves the *interpretation* of sensory data that we are so prone to perceptual mistakes. The basis for error is compound: we may misinterpret cause and effect (the child is bored because he is too dull to understand the lesson); or we may totally misjudge the situation (the children *seem* attentive and are therefore not bored). Our perceptions, in short, lead us to assume that what we *think* to be so, *is* so.

An occurrence during the experiment serves as an illustration. In the teacher conversations which invariably take place at the end of a semester, when classes are reassigned, a teacher received some advance warning from a colleague. One of the incoming third-graders, a boy named Will, had been something of a behavior problem in the second grade. He talked incessantly, constantly was out of his seat, and frequently clashed with other youngsters. Another boy in the same class, Tim, had also distinguished himself by his exceptional fondness for school, agreeable nature, and the special pleasure he took in helping the teacher.

At the end of summer vacation, in one of those inadvertent errors that happen now and then, the third-grade instructor confused the two names. He mistakenly assumed that Tim was the sinner, and Will the saint. Acting upon this misconception, he watched Tim carefully, constantly admonished him to stay in his seat, and repeatedly warned that any unnecessary conversation would be penalized. As part of the same confusion, Will was accepted warmly, praised for commendable behavior, and given considerable latitude.

In a matter of weeks, Tim's previously exemplary conduct deteriorated. He developed a habit of whispering, furtively, during seatwork; wandered about the room whenever the opportunity arose; and produced lackluster homework. Will, in contrast, became something of a model student: he worked diligently, cooperated with his classmates, anticipated the teacher's wishes, and no longer was a disruption. Teachers, in brief, often find exactly what they are looking for.

Children differ not only in their capacities, their learning modes, and their personalities, but also in their emotional systems. The effectiveness of the teacher-student relationship therefore rests on the degree of correctness with which one "reads" the other. Adulthood and childhood, after all, are different worlds, and teachers must, through empathy, deduction, and intuition, seek to understand their students.[6] More often than not, clashes between teacher and learner stem from mutual misperceptions, which cause one or the other to respond to the wrong cues. Such misperceptions may also diminish an important by-product of schooling: the opportunity for students to acquire a habit of success and an ability to manage their emotional affairs. We sometimes forget that schools teach more than subject matter; although the lesson may involve geography or history, the child will also learn that he is competent or incompetent, liked or unliked, successful or unsuccessful—attitudes of mind which sink deep into the undercurrents of the psyche.

There is, as a result, a profound need for better "perceptual training" in teacher education. Faulty judgment, for example, occurs frequently whenever there is a sharp contrast in the racial or class background of teacher and student. This is not to say, of course, that middle-class black teachers should not work with lower-class white children, or that a middle-class white teacher ought not to teach an upper-class black child. Rather, it is to say that we seek what our experiences have taught us to look for, and we are more likely to find the expected than the unexpected; in a sense we are all "impulsive perceivers." If new experiences do not demonstrate the subjectivity of our perceptions, we can carry on in our mistaken impressions indefinitely.

Master teachers are distinguished by their sensitivity to the tricky quirks of personality and to the special rhythms of the individual child. They seem to take keen interest in the particular personality of each student. For when children are viewed as idiosyncratic entities, rather than as an amorphous group, the approach to teaching alters. Precisely the same attitude distinguishes the general medical practitioner, interested in the overall welfare of his patients, from the specialist who treats not the individual, but an infected ear or a sprained ankle.

All of the teachers in the artistry program wished their students to behave properly and to learn the assigned material. The best, however, took little for granted. They probed beneath surface behavior to learn more about the understructure of their student's compulsions. They sought to understand each child's private world. When learning problems developed, they tried to determine whether the difficulty rested with the student or the instruction.

Base your control of learning activities on student behavior—another important way in which artist teachers differ from ordinary ones. No two students, classes, or schools are the same. Teaching methods, time allotments, incentives, and evaluative tactics, therefore, must fit each situation. Artistic teaching requires behavioral reciprocity; the teacher adjusts his or her behavior to that of the learner. Such adjustments influence the rate at which material is introduced, the accommodations made for individual differences among students, the amount of reinforcement, the nature and depth of teacher questions, and the form of instructional feedback. Teaching, to repeat an earlier point, is an interactive craft. It is for this reason that battle-scarred veterans advise neophytes to "teach the student, not the subject." But to do so, the teacher must perceive and communicate accurately.

Communication problems occur when teachers and students misconstrue each other's aspirations and motives. Countless youngsters view the teacher as villain, and large numbers of teachers believe children have a natural penchant for foolishness and mischief. While both teachers and students are susceptible to perceptual error, the responsibility for remediation falls upon teachers if only because they alone have the power to rectiify matters. Teachers must, through practice, learn to judge their students accurately and, conversely, to take steps which ensure that they themselves are correctly understood by their students. To facilitate this, it is necessary that teachers gain insight into their own inclinations toward distortion. Teachers, then, must make a deliberate effort to become adept at "reading" classroom situations and "perceiving" individual students. The line separating an alienated student from a bored one is delicate. Indeed, perceptual errors are commonplace among even sensitive teachers; among insensitive ones, they are inevitable. Finally, teachers need to develop techniques which can be used to improve teacher-student empathy—so that both have a better understanding of classroom situations.

To control the communication problems resulting from perceptual error, it is sometimes advantageous to have several teachers periodically evaluate a child's progress. Multiple judgments are common practice in graduate schools; they might be equally appropriate in elementary and secondary schools. Too, more use could be made of scheduling arrangements which permit a better "match" between students and teachers. The administrative complexities, admittedly, would be a bit more severe, but since students' achievement is significantly affected by the way they relate to their teachers, striving for maximum compatibility would seem worthwhile. To assume that any student can learn effectively with any teacher is to fall prey to a seductive fallacy: "personality conflicts" between teachers and students are not baseless illusions; they are the normal consequences of human interchange.

It should be remembered, moreover, that our methods of estimating aptitude are relatively primitive and subject to considerable error. Raw ability, as noted earlier, is tempered by a number of other factors—motivation, persistence, endurance, and so on. The instances in which a child's ability to learn has been misjudged by the school are legion. Moreover, the consequences of such labels as "fast learner" or "slow learner" are seductive since, in teaching, what we expect to occur in the way of achievement usually does occur. Knowing this, experienced teachers will occasionally confront their students with tasks slightly above their presumed ability.

Concentrate on a few dominant goals, central to your purpose. Every teacher is obliged to cover assigned curriculum and develop designated skills and knowledge. Artist teachers pursue, in addition, collateral targets, further enriching the intellectual mix. They incorporate teaching objectives they especially value which cut across a variety of subject matter. A superb teacher in Vancouver, for example, sees to it that every child has a substantial exposure to logical reasoning. Another, in Louisiana, makes sure that all her students thoroughly grasp the essentials of good nutrition.

These are special goals—part of the teacher's personal ethos—which imbue teaching with extra significance. They are closely tied to professional pride and self-expectation. Accomplishing these goals somehow makes teaching more rewarding and helps to counter the extraordinary pressures associated with today's classrooms.

Since potential cannot be predicted with any exactness, an opportunity to test one's power against a challenge—even at the risk of failure—would seem to be a child's inalienable right. One often encounters students who, having had just such an opportunity, graduate from college despite the fact that their high schools considered them "slow" or "not college material." Artist teachers, I discovered, are inclined to be open-minded about a learner's aptitude and to expect the most rather than the least.

Moreover, no one knows from what mysterious provenance comes that serendipitous moment when an idea is formed. Perception can develop slowly and methodically, as with Einstein's field theory, or in a sudden insight, as when Helen Keller discovered that "everything has a name." Comprehension sometimes begins with a sliver of light, illuminating a dark corner of the path, sometimes with an unexpected luminescence making all clear. A chance remark may become the irritant grain of sand that eventually grows into a pearl. Who knows which child will become the Chapman's *Homer* for some undetected Keats. Understanding—the realization of structural order—creates its own special euphoria.

The artistry program demonstrated five primary sources of perceptual error. First, children and teachers do not always share the same set of values. Exposure to ethnic differences, to the customs of different subcultures, and to varying beliefs about the purposes of education are still largely ignored in teacher training. Teachers, moreover, are prepared for service not in a particular school, or with a particular socioeconomic group, but for a mythical "average school." Thus, they sometimes do not really understand the children they teach. Insularity is endemic in our pattern of social stratification: there are black children in Miami who have never played on its beaches and Puerto Ricans in New York who have never set foot on Park Avenue, just as there are white teachers commuting to poverty area schools who have never seen the inside of a ghetto dwelling. Moreover, the customs of the profession are such that the newest teachers, and often the least skillful, frequently are assigned to schools serving minority children with divergent cultural attitudes and beliefs. In these situations, the likelihood of teacher-learner misperceptions increases sharply.

There is, in sum, a double bind: if teachers do not understand the cultures which have conditioned their children, they can neither be responsive to them nor reckon with their scheme of values; without awareness of a child's values, perceptual accuracy is virtually impossible. We found, as a general rule, that the more worldly the teacher—worldly in the sense of social consciousness and sophistication—the more likely close attention would be paid to cultural and ethnic differences and the teaching would have vitality and relevance.

Second, in coping with the nuances of the classroom, teachers often make faulty inferences. Deciphering problems in learning is a precarious matter. One can make an inferential mistake because of a private prejudice, because one responds to the wrong clues or misinterprets the right ones, or because one fails to recognize the clues as they become manifest. Prolonged silence in a child, as a case in point, may stem from sullenness or indifference, but quietness and withdrawal are also prompted by many other things. It is tempting to assume that the articulate child is learning and that the inarticulate one is not. In truth, however, fluency and comprehension are not exact corollaries of one another.

A third source of error is attributable to the habit children learn early in their school careers of camouflaging their real feelings. Even the dullest of students soon recognize that they can deceive a teacher by simply wearing an attentive look in class. Once the face signals interest, tedium can be alleviated by rich excursions into one's private fantasy. Teachers, it might be added, often cooperate in such deception by being gullible. Avoiding deception by probing beneath surface appearances and asking pointed questions is a mark of superior pedagogy. Indeed, one of the distinguishing benchmarks of the gifted teacher is the ability to go beyond the obvious in order to discover where the learner's mind really is.

Fourth, the misinterpretation of classroom phenomena is perpetuated by contradictions between student and teacher objectives. Teachers, in the main, are chiefly interested in how much their classes accomplish. Students, on the other hand, are frequently impelled by entirely different motives. They often learn not because they regard the learning as useful, but because high grades, symbolizing academic success, bring other rewards. Youngsters may, for example, prize the teacher's approval, wish to please their parents, or—out of sheer competitiveness—seek to outdo their classmates. When student objectives, for whatever reason, are incongruent with those of the teacher, the probability of faulty communication rises.

Such difficulties are not insurmountable. Perceptual errors can be reduced through training which provides a surer knowledge of the learner's out-of-school environment; through systematic practice in analyzing classroom events; and through a calculated effort by the teacher to verify initial impressions. Some for example, accept their first conclusions as fact without bothering to look for corroborating evidence. Others assess, and reassess, in order to be sure.

It might also be observed, in this regard, that the teachers with minimal command of their subjects are most prone to perceptual inaccuracy. The reason, of course, is that when predominant attention must be given to the substance of the lesson, it is impossible to focus on anything else. There is a considerable difference in the kind of teaching that goes on when the teacher has an intimate acquaintance with the topic of the lesson. If teachers are genuinely knowledgeable, if they know their subjects well enough to discriminate between the central ideas and the secondary matter, and if they can take the intellectual ideas beyond what is in the textbook, the quality of the pedagogy is greatly increased. It is only when the teacher has a thorough grasp of the material, moreover, that different dimensions of teaching can be utilized effectively.

Devote as much time as possible to whatever you enjoy most in teaching. Artist teachers do not leave their professional gratification to chance but handle their assignments in ways they find satisfying. Teaching is a complex, multidimensional pursuit, and most instructional tasks can be accomplished through a variety of means. Six kinds of teaching, for example, are widely used:

1. *Explanatory Teaching.* The teacher explains particular aspects of a lesson objective: How decimals are converted to percentage; or the reasons why societies have codes of behavior; or the process through which oil is extracted from corn.
2. *Inspiratory Teaching.* The teacher prompts engagement in the learning activity: "Why not describe your reaction to the new law in a short essay"; or, "Let's review the main ideas together"; or, "You might want to prepare for the test early!"

3. *Informative Teaching.* The teacher conveys information, usually through verbal statements: "The three primary factors contributing to the war were poverty, public unrest, and political fear." Or, "Hong Kong has a thriving economy and is a major financial center."

4. *Corrective Teaching.* The teacher analyzes student work, diagnoses errors, and offers corrective advice: "Your mistake is forgetting to capitalize proper nouns"; or, "It's a lovely poem but the meter may be off a bit"; or, "Try to keep your eye on the ball when you're kicking!"

5. *Interactive Teaching.* The teacher, through dialogue and questioning, increases learner understanding: "Why do you suppose Switzerland worries about national defense?" Or, "Would it be dangerous to form an alliance with Italy, but not with Germany?" Interactive teaching can underscore an idea the teacher wishes to emphasize, or facilitate students' development of their own ideas: "How can you portray your concept of color relationships graphically?"

6. *Programmatic Teaching.* The teacher does not instruct, per se, but instead guides the student's activity so that self-instruction occurs: "Read the author's description of changing social values and decide whether you agree." Or, "Put your points in outline form and arrange them in the sequence you think best."

Teachers tend to favor one kind of teaching over another, and to be especially adept at particular techniques. Thus, when choices exist between alternative methods of accomplishing an objective, it is sensible to follow personal preference, as long as good results are obtained. Using preferred methods generally reduces fatigue, increases job satisfaction, and enhances success. While the worst of teachers depend almost entirely on one approach, and while artist teachers are usually good at all six kinds of teaching, the presumption that teachers should be equally fond of each technique is obviously senseless.

Fifth, misconceptions also abound when students do not "hear" the teacher correctly. They may misunderstand directions, "read" nonverbal cues improperly, or fail to grasp the purpose of the activity. Their problem is not an inability to learn, but rather an inability to grasp what the teacher wants. They simply do not know what is going on. In time, as failure piles upon failure, they no longer care. One senses in these circumstances that both teacher and student are imprisoned by fate: were it not for the rules of the game both would prefer to be elsewhere, doing other things. Such situations are made all the more deplorable by their striking contrast with classrooms where the communication is so clear, the goals so inviting, and the learning excitement so high, that the children almost seem to revel in their tasks.

The perceptual attributes of the teacher are of very great importance. Neither a pedant nor a therapist suffices, for the former maligns the spirit and the latter favors emotional comfort at the cost of an uninformed mind. What we must have are teachers who know both their subjects and their students, who have the essential pedagogical and interpersonal skills essential to their intent, and who are themselves positive, informed, and observant. Teacher training has traditionally centered on substance and method. In view, however, of the enormous liabilities which stem from false perceptions, fully as much attention must be given in the preservice and inservice education of teachers to perceptual skills as to knowledge and technique.

RECAPITULATION

Accurate perception is critical in teaching. Moreover, perception is a two-way street: to reduce misunderstanding the teacher must both communicate accurately and decipher student behavior correctly.

Perception, therefore, involves dual skills—picking up on clues and decoding their meaning. Both are developed through deliberate practice; both, consequently, are self-learned. The teacher must speculate about what is going on, and why, as well as verify the correctness of the inferences. Sustained effort to understand cause and effect, and to know why certain things happen, eventually leads to perceptiveness.

Once teachers acquire well-developed perceptual skills, they function at a considerable advantage. They are able, for example, to organize teaching-learning activities more shrewdly. They can respond to student behavior with much greater sensitivity. And, importantly, they can anticipate potential problems well in advance and take preventive steps.

Perception is facilitated by deduction, intuition, and empathy—identifying with children's concerns. When the teacher analyzes classroom situations, looks beneath surface behavior, and seeks to determine why students behave as they do, insight deepens. Lastly, perception improves when teachers have a firm grasp of their subjects, when they are familiar with their students' out-of-school lives, and when they accumulate "behavioral data" and process it rapidly.

SOME ISSUES

1. Can teachers develop perceptual acuity away from students, by, for example, practicing with case studies, or must they develop it through actual classroom experience?
2. If teaching is an interactive art involving "behavioral reciprocity," what training promotes such interpersonal skills?
3. What preparation enables teachers to use perceptual knowledge in scheduling classroom time, reviewing concepts, and making judgments about test scores?

5

∽

ARTISTRY AND INTUITION

One of the distinguishing characteristics of artist teachers is their periodic use of intuitive thinking, particularly in making quick decisions. When there is a deliberate effort to "read" the signs which are present in a classroom situation, and to form the clues into a functional pattern, rapid and accurate inference is often possible. At times, moreover, swiftness can be almost as important as depth in decision making.[1]

Intuition is of great significance in teaching because pedagogy, as noted earlier, is an interpersonal craft. The artist's colors, the poet's words, the sculptor's clay, and the musician's notes are inanimate. In contrast, children—the teacher's medium—are reactive. As in a chess match, the moves of one player are influenced by those of the other.

Because of this interplay, in a typical day teachers make scores of instructional judgments: Should the day-dreaming student be called to task or ignored? Which would be preferable, an oral or written test? Would it be wiser to take time from English or social studies to explain the new fire drill rules? Is it better to be compassionate or dispassionate when a child is overcome with frustration? Such questions, occurring in the midst of the action, usually are resolved impulsively. Careful deliberation is impossible, and the teacher therefore seizes on the course that seems most sensible.

Intuition is essential in teaching, moreover, because much instruction involves monitoring and appraising learner understanding. No special clairvoyance is needed to discern that a child is having trouble. Locating the cause of the trouble, however, can be quite another matter. Few teachers escape the dismay that arises upon discovering—after much time wasted on the wrong things—that obvious keys to the real problem were overlooked.

Intuition, it might also be added, helps to organize cognition. Shaped by perception and knowledge, it serves to coalesce the two. Confronted with a dilemma—whether to end or continue an animated classroom discussion—the teacher makes a rapid assessment, assimilates the available cues, and forms a conclusion.

It is intuition, furthermore, which nurtures the skill Jacob Kounin labeled "with-it-ness."[2] The extraordinary awareness displayed by exceptional teachers comes, in large part, from their constant effort to piece together meaning out of fragmentary detail.

Make use of intuition and hunch in modifying routine practices. Artist teachers who seem, so often, to do exactly the right thing at exactly the right time have well-tempered instincts. They use insight, acquired through long experience, to get at the heart of a matter and sense what will work. They not only prefer to obey these instincts but are uneasy when, for some reason, they must disregard them. Such teachers find instinctive knowledge exceedingly useful, readily accessible, and an effective shortcut in reaching conclusions.

The importance of intuition in teaching became evident on two occasions during the experiments. First, when the teachers were testing their theater-related pedagogical inventions, they sometimes reported that a particular maneuver was unworkable. Since many of these rejected tactics seemed, at least on the surface, rather good, an effort was made in subsequent discussions to ascertain the cause of the failure. As a result of these conversations, I began to suspect that it was not the invention which was faulty, but rather the way in which it was used. Many of the teachers had sufficient skill and knowledge to devise an interesting strategy, but they often deployed it in the wrong way or at an inappropriate time.

The problem arose again in conjunction with the creativity exercises. Some teachers, though extremely able, had undue difficulty. They were unable to judge when an unproductive idea should be abandoned, and frequently had trouble predicting what would, or would not, be successful. To learn why these problems persisted, I again talked with some of the participants at length. Ultimately, I concluded that many teachers make almost no use of their intuitive abilities. This was cause for concern because there was already considerable evidence that intuition is an important factor in artistry, as the following example illustrates:

Disturbed about a child's semester-long disinterest in school, a teacher—apparently out of nowhere—was taken by an unusual notion. She asked the student to become the "teacher of the day," a role presumably created on the spot, and to teach, on the following Friday, the rules of subject-verb agreement. The maneuver, happily, was successful. After some preparation and a bit of teacher assistance, the child presented the lesson with reasonable effectiveness. Then, "turned-on," he remained actively involved in the other classwork. Elated, the teacher thought about the incident and wondered why it had taken her fifteen weeks to come to her senses. What gave rise to the teacher's impulse? Although it was unpremeditated, something caused her to suspect it might succeed. The inspiration, possibly, was intuitive; a few nebulous clues, grasped through some sort of shrewd perception, led the teacher to her brilliant stroke.

The ability to use intuition is based on two crucial skills. It is important to know what kind of information to look for, and equally critical to grasp its true meaning. Most teachers are better at one than the other. Some, for example, have an ingrained feel for the hints that will be most helpful. Others lack this ability but, instead, are good at sifting through seemingly trivial information and finding something significant. Apparently, the old adage still holds: using one's strong points tends to further debilitate weak ones.

These premises suggest that teachers can perhaps sharpen their intuitive faculties and use them more fully. After a few years in the classroom, sophistication increases, there is a greater sensitivity to the problems of pedagogy, and the subtleties of the art gradually become more clear. Once this happens, teachers can often convert their insights into intellectual rules of thumb, or cognitive shortcuts. As a result, quicker, and often better, instructional judgments are possible.

Intuition, psychologists tell us, is "quick or ready apprehension"—knowledge gained without recourse to inference or reason. What this implies is that we can know things—and make use of them—without understanding precisely how they were learned. Indeed, we often may not know that we are aware of something; and yet the knowledge is reflected in our behavior. A teacher may sense, for example, that a student is insecure and, without any conscious thought, provide more support than usual.

Instructional judgments are formed through a variety of cognitive processes. Some judgments are the result of logical reasoning. For example, teachers frequently decide, on the basis of test data, that the class is ready for the next level of work. They reason in linear, sequenced fashion, processing their information, and ultimately reach a conclusion. Such judgments can be made slowly or quickly, depending upon how rapidly the successive steps are taken.

Other instructional judgments are based on acquired knowledge and repeated experience. Early in a teacher's career they are performed consciously. Beginning teachers, for example, make it a point to remind the children about putting the learning materials away before dismissal. Later, such instructional directives become a kind of conditioned reflex and are made mechanically, without conscious awareness.

Instructional judgments are intuitive. These are not the result of conscious or preconscious functions. Rather they are based on accumulated insight and induced by sensory perception. Often the teacher is uncertain as to how the conclusion was reached. Intuitive judgments come, in the words of the dictionary, from "the quick perception of truth without conscious attention or reasoning."

We use the words *hunch* and *guess* to describe these kinds of judgments. They evolve from obscure innuendoes in the classroom situation which are somehow divined and interpreted. Impetuously, for example, a teacher decides to delay the beginning of a new unit until the following week. Plans have been made, everything is in readiness, the students are waiting, but something "tells" her that the time is not quite right. The intangible "something" is buried in the learning milieu, and perceived in some vague, imprecise, way.

Much of teaching involves an effort to overcome specific learning problems. Teachers must appraise a situation and make rational judgments. All teachers, however, do not form their conclusions in the same way; some examine the problem carefully and make systematic deductions. Others leap rapidly to a prospective solution, test it, and if it fails, search for something else. The first approach is orderly and regulated, leading after a period of time to a well-considered determination. The second, in contrast, is a good deal more random: the teacher moves abruptly from one idea to another until something works.

Many psychologists believe that each of us has a preferred way of thinking. Our tendency to reason in stepwise fashion, or to jump from one possibility to another, is inherent in our nature. Some of us, in short, are pedagogical gamblers—betting with our hunches—and some of us are not.

Sequential reasoning and intuition operate differently but fulfill the same function and often produce similar conclusions. The major difference is that intuitive judgments, while more erratic and less controlled, offer greater economy of motion—conclusions are reached quickly, without prolonged deliberation. Each, of course, has its special advantages and each is particularly useful in certain situations. Interestingly enough, however, many teachers avoid intuitive thinking, perhaps because they were taught that it is unreliable.

Intuitions compress relevant detail into usable guidelines, allowing us to summarize a situation in relatively short order. Intuitive judgments are also helpful in two additional ways. They can be used to identify possibilities, and once something is under way, they can be used to confirm, or disaffirm, its correctness. As Jerome Bruner has said, ''An anticipatory intuition can manifest itself not only in cases where information is lacking, but also in cases where all the information is available, to be organized before a solution can be embarked upon.''[3] Seeking the answer to a problem, we may find a particularly good prospect if we allow our minds to toy with various ideas. We can then appraise the merits of each. The initial inspiration, whether called foresight or precognition, is a *directional* intuition. *Corroborating* intuitions, in contrast, occur after a judgment has been made. They serve, mainly, to tell us whether we are on the right track.

All of these intuitive procedures require repeated exposure. It is highly unlikely that a surgeon, with little knowledge of auto-mobiles, would intuitively know what to do about a defective generator. A skilled mechanic, in contrast, could probably diag-nose the problem in a few seconds. Beginning teachers, as another illustration, frequently have difficulty with classroom control. Yet the theories of classroom management are well known, and the specific techniques through which veteran teachers maintain order are easily identified. Neither lecture, nor textbook, nor memorized rules, however, enable neophytes to handle a class adroitly. It is only after sustained practice that intuitive understanding matures. Intuitions, in short, are dependent upon acquired acumen: without adequate background, the "quick cognitive leap" is vir-tually impossible.

Ironically, in our youth many of us were taught to avoid guessing. In point of fact, however, we often find ourselves in positions where we must act before we know enough to act in-telligently. Hence, speculation—leading to intuitive insight—is sometimes the only sensible course available.

Intuitive thinking, it should be noted, is neither a matter of luck nor special gift. It is a part of ordinary intelligence, crystal-ized and sharpened by experience. As familiarity in a repetitive endeavor accumulates, our intuitive capacities are refined through practice. And as we become familar with typical situa-tions, we recognize similar patterns. Thus, through stored in-sight, we often can accelerate the judgmental process by taking advantage of cognitive step-savers.

It would be a mistake to view intuitive thinking as a conve-nient short-cut for the lazy. Used in the right ways, it can be a powerful pedagogical tool. In fact, the ability to make quick judgments effectively, so as to reduce error when decisions must be reached rapidly, may be more important in teaching than we think.

Artist teachers are far better decision makers than their ordi-nary counterparts. They seem, more often than not, to make the right "guesses." In so doing, however, they rely more on in-tuitive sense than on set rules. They appear to assess a situation in one quick take, activate some sort of internal computer, and respond in ways which—upon later analysis—are remarkably canny. The intuition on which they depend, however, has been developed and sharpened over time.

As a consequence of these assumptions, efforts to stimulate intuitive thinking were initiated during the experiments. As in the creativity training, the exercises centered around the teachers' daily involvements. The participants were asked, first, to think about classroom judgments they habitually needed to make, and to identify those that were most troublesome. To sharpen the focus, a short handout was distributed listing areas which, according to research findings, were particularly vulnerable to error: diagnosing learning problems, coping with misbehavior, making pacing decisions, and utilizing reinforcement opportunities.

Next, the teachers were given a simple scheme for practicing intuitive predictions. The scheme involved five steps:

1. Choose a teaching situation where predictions are possible.
2. Find as many clues as you can.
3. Make a prediction.
4. Later, when possible, check the accuracy of your prediction.
5. Review the situation, looking for clues you may have overlooked or misjudged.

Then the teachers were asked to speculate about a series of cause-and-effect situations in classrooms. The one replicated below, for example, was typical:

BE INTUITIVE

In a small school in rural Nebraska, a teacher taught a fifth grade unit on farming and then one on banking. Although the children were more interested in the farming unit, their test scores were far better on the banking. This seemed odd since the teacher used the same methods, scheduled similar amounts of time, and followed the Teacher's Manual recommendations in both units. Moreover, each test was prepared by the textbook publisher. The only differences were that, in the farming unit, class discussion came before the reading assignment whereas in the banking unit it came afterwards; in the farming unit some time was devoted to analyzing and comparing the practices of local farmers; and the banking unit was taught before the art activity while, in the case of the farming unit, art took place first. Another oddity was that—although the test scores were higher in banking—the discussions were a good deal more lively in farming.

1. Why did the children like the farming unit better?
2. Why did they get higher scores on the banking test?
3. Why were the discussions more animated in farming?

There were no mandatory responses, of course, but I was pleased when teachers suggested that the preference for the farming unit was attributable to the school's agrarian environment; that the higher scores on banking stemmed from the fact that time was not taken from the study of the text for a consideration of local practices, and, conversely, the farming discussions were more lively because time *was* given to a matter of community interest.

Not all of the teachers embraced intuitive thinking with a passion, but many of those who did were permanently hooked. A young man, for example, became so enamored that he developed an intuition unit for his own fourth graders. Several of the children, I was told, began to predict the outcome of sporting events; a few became amateur weather forecasters; and one boy developed considerable skill in guessing the weight of his schoolmates.

Another teacher, an exceedingly intelligent woman in her fifties, was especially memorable. Because of her extreme interest in intuition, I spend a good deal of time conversing with her. She was convinced that we have an "intuitive state"—a time when we are particularly open to the perception of inconspicuous detail. There were periods during the day, she said, when she was more alert than usual. During these periods, she could—by concentrating on a situation—increase her receptivity and form impressions which facilitated intuitive judgment. On one occasion, she showed me a piece of paper on which she had jotted down an example of an intuitive state, immediately after it occurred. She had been talking with a child whose homework was invariably poor. She asked the youngster if he did his homework at a customary time and place, if he found it easy to understand, and if he thought it important. He nodded affirmatively to each of these questions. Then, on impulse, for no reason she could identify, she suddenly asked him if he sometimes had fantasies about football, when doing homework. He looked at her with astonishment and said yes.

Another incident involved a teacher who, at the time, was exceedingly angry with his principal. The teacher received a negative administrator evaluation at the end of the previous semester. He challenged the report, pointing out that the principal had spent very little time in his room. The principal retorted that he could glance at a room (the classroom doors in this school had small glass windows in the upper panel) and know in a few seconds whether the instruction was good or bad. The teacher, understandably, regarded this claim as absurd.

The intuition exercises reminded him of the principal's remark and his own bitterness. For some strange reasons, he took to looking in the classrooms of his friends, when he happened to be in the halls, to see if he could get a sense of what was going on. Later, in the staff room or cafeteria, he would explain his behavior, apologize, and sometimes ask a question or two to verify a perception. There were two outcomes: one, he was promptly dubbed ''The Peeper'' by his colleagues, and two, he discovered that, after a little practice, he could occasionally form a surprisingly accurate impression of what had just transpired, or was about to occur. I shared the teacher's objection to the principal's thoughtlessness and egotism, but the intuitive judgments he learned to make were interesting.

As the exercises progressed, individual preference for either linear thinking or intuitive ''hunching'' was mainly unchanged. Those favoring systematic reasoning relied principally on step-by-step analysis, and the hunchers continued their leaps. But two significant differences were apparent: (1) both types gathered a larger amount of perceptual data to help them in their decision making, and (2) the linear thinkers began to make more use of their intuitive abilities than before. To the extent that these informal findings are valid, we can assume that a predilection for either intuitive or linear thought is imbedded in personality. Nonetheless, problem-solving and decision-making skills improve when there is greater perception of situational details.

A carefully designed program of self-development in the use of intuitive capacities might have considerable value. The fact that most of the teachers found the exercises beneficial and gradually became more adept at rapid classroom judgments supports the presumption that intuitive thinking is learnable. Even the most skeptical of the participants, for example, eventually recognized that intuitive thought is not counterfeit, but rather a different kind of perceptual system.

It also became clear that a place exists for both linear and intuitive thought in teaching. There is a time for following carefully worked out plans and a time for yielding to sudden insight. Intuition seems most useful when the problem is vague and nebulous; when the problem is obvious, systematic analysis may have more to offer. In any event, it can scarcely be denied that intuition has received scant attention in the education of teachers.

A case could be made, one suspects, for training in stochastic pedagogy—instruction guided by "informed guesses" when no other guidelines are available. Teaching, like some other human endeavors, must often proceed by guesswork. The painter must somehow divine whether further strokes of the brush will weaken rather than strengthen the painting, just as a chef must speculate whether or not the sauce has reached its ultimate perfection. And a physician, forced to choose between two drugs—both of which have negative side effects—must sometimes gamble. If, then, a degree of guessing is inevitable in teaching, it would seem sensible to develop greater intuitive capability.

RECAPITULATION

Artist teachers use intuitive decision making more than other teachers. Recognizing that there are limits to rationality, they believe a "feel for what is right" often is more productive than prolonged analysis.

Intuitive decision making is considerably faster than linear thinking, permitting greater economy of motion as well as the possibility of acting "while the iron is hot." The ability to make quick, effective decisions, consequently, is extremely useful in teaching.

Intuitive thinking is learnable through experience and a careful effort to process perceptual evidence. By actively looking for clues, speculating about their meaning, and testing the resulting hunches, intuitive thought is cultivated. In making intuitive decisions, attention is focused on the total problem rather than on an isolated part. Practiced regularly, it produces intellectual rules of thumb which facilitate teaching efficiency.

Intuitions are also helpful in other ways. They provide directional signals, indicating new possibilities and giving early warnings when a chosen path is not likely to be successful. While intuitive and linear thought are both necessary in teaching, the use of inference has not been given as much attention as it perhaps deserves. Stochastic teaching—instruction guided by "informed guesses" when no other guidelines are available—appears to be an equally neglected art.

SOME ISSUES

1. What instincts can be developed for improving intuitive action?
2. Can teachers with a preference for linear decision making make use of their intuitive apparatus?
3. Can the ability to make accurate inferences about teaching situations be developed?

6

ARTISTRY AND THE MASTERY OF PEDAGOGICAL PRINCIPLES

Efficient lessons are often the mark of artist teachers. Working with faculties, I was impressed repeatedly with the astonishing disparity in accomplishment. As I sat in classrooms and talked with teachers, I gradually realized that some maneuvers are a good deal more expedient than others, and that excellent teachers are particularly distinguished by their ability to organize an efficient classroom.

Expeditious teaching seems to be associated with four special talents: (1) recognizing logical linkages, (2) choosing efficient procedures, (3) anticipating impediments, and (4) exploiting latent resources. The first talent involves recognizing the natural correspondence between two instructional goals. Mathematics, for example, can easily be incorporated in a science experiment. The study of adjectives dovetails nicely with the improvement of writing skill. Critical thinking blends perfectly with the analysis of current events in social studies. An expert teacher recognizes these linkages and uses them advantageously.

In addition to seeing linkages, artistic teachers seem able to choose procedures which accomplish their objectives with dispatch. Schooling is burdened with a great number of obligations. Students are expected to learn prescribed subject matter, sound values, social graces, and—in the best of situations—the skills of reflective thought. Virtually every teacher wants to fulfill these expectations as circumstances permit. To do so, choices must be made regarding the amount of time that can be devoted to any particular aim. In teaching about the causes of the Korean War, for example, the necessary information can be extracted from a textbook, delivered by lecture, or acquired through some form of dialectic learning wherein the teacher, through discussion, helps the class grasp the major concepts. Which method is best depends upon the time that can be afforded, the teaching energy which must be reserved for other matters, the fatigue quotient of the learners, and the importance attached to the topic. To a very large extent, the effective use of method determines whether the learning will be successful or unsuccessful.

Preferences among procedural options stem from style, belief, and commitment. They are closely related to artistic teaching in two ways: first, an unwise choice hampers students, no matter how adept the teacher is in its use; second, a tactically wise choice that is badly executed also limits attainment. Artistry is at its peak when the teacher chooses efficient procedures and implements them adroitly.

Far too little attention is devoted to the relationship between means and ends in teaching. One of the unexpected benefits of the artistry project was that it required teachers to think, far more deeply than usual, about what they wanted to do and about different ways of achieving their goals. When teachers ponder their intentions carefully, many alternatives come to mind and options which best fit individual inclination and aim can then be selected. But when time is not taken to think through a teaching problem, the range of choices seems minimal. Artistry, then, requires a willingness to speculate about an instructional situation until a series of tactics becomes apparent.

The interesting thing about instructional choice is that judgment gleaned from experience is transferable. During the project, the teachers played with one problem at a time. There were no deadlines; ideas could be revised or discarded after tentative try-outs, and the effects of alternative procedures could be compared. As a result, perceptions of teaching-learning phenomena—the effect of teachers' actions on student achievement—gradually increased. The teachers often found, moreover, that a principle which evolved could later be applied in a totally different context. It may well be that procedural choice and artistic judgment in teaching are cumulative. Gifted teachers progressively refine their discriminatory ability.

The third of the special aptitudes has to do with anticipating impediments. To teach expediently, one must recognize in advance, before motion is wasted, that the timing is wrong, or that the materials must be simplified, or that the drill is unsuitable.

In one of the project schools, for example, the sixth-grade instructors were told by the district administration to extend the language arts curriculum with a unit in which the students created an original story. A teacher—who also happened to be part of the artistry experiment—was bothered by the mandate. Her class had recently finished a series of written assignments in social studies; the students were not avid writers; they were tired of "creating," and she was certain they would react to the additional language arts assignment with hostility. She knew she could force them to comply, but since a sampling of stories would be collected by district administrators for evaluation, it was important that the students do their best work.

The difficulty was overcome, with elegant simplicity, through a combination of two dimensions of artistry: the anticipation of a problem and the invention of a solution. First, the teacher saw immediately that an additional writing assignment would sour the class, because the timing was wrong; and second, she was able to circumvent the impediment with an imaginative strategy.

She advised the class that she had decided to produce a book of stories for the third-grade children. Every student would have time to examine library books for eight-year olds; study typical vocabulary; and choose an appropriate theme. Each student, moreover, was to decide upon illustrations and construct rough sketches. The stories selected for inclusion in the book would be illustrated by students especially good at art, or by the authors themselves. Every story would be read by one third-grader, and judged for appeal and overall quality. The twelve best stories would be bound in book form, and placed in the library's collection.

Upon finding a functional purpose to the story writing, the sixth-grade class was strongly motivated. Capturing the interest of the primary children became something of a challenge, and several of the brightest students were bitterly disappointed when their story was not selected. The preferences of the third graders, in fact, surprised virtually everyone.

An unskilled teacher has no way of knowing what will or will not work. A skilled one, in contrast, makes use of an internal sensing apparatus and avoids having to start over because something is unworkable. Some teachers can determine, in a few swift glances, whether some instructional materials will appeal to their students. Others must try them out before reaching a conclusion. A bungling practitioner frequently misjudges readiness: the next level of work is started too soon or too late. An apt one perceives when the time is right. An aptitude for accurate anticipation, in sum, is a major asset.

No teacher can overcome every detrimental circumstance that arises. A prolonged period of inclement weather, excitement over a special event about to occur, student empathy for a classmate who has been reprimanded, anxiety over a test, all take their toll. But such things are generally exceptions to the day-by-day scene. In the normal run of events, effective teachers are able to pick techniques which offer the greatest hope.

Find the most efficient and expedient ways of getting things done. This seems to be sensible and seemingly simple advice, but it is more difficult than one might suspect. Efficiency is related to high expectations, since one makes the other possible. A passion for excellence, however, is also essential. Without a concern for quality, striving for efficiency and expediency can result in a quicker, but poorer, product. Much of artistry lies in doing ordinary things with efficacy and deftness.

Although the most successful of teachers share a common set of attributes—cheerfulness, a conspicuous fondness for children, a love for the subject matter they teach, and a caring demeanor—they also excel in choosing sensible human management procedures. Here prescription is once again ineffectual: one cannot be programmed in advance to make deft judgments in controlling children's behavior. Expert teachers have a seasoned sense of when to do what: they seem to apply pressure, or ease off, at the right time. Depending upon circumstances, they may choose to either overlook a slight rule infraction or call a student to task. They have a way of knowing which students must be pushed and which must be led.[1]

Expediency has a place in classroom management as well. Supplies can be passed out in five minutes or fifteen; attendance takes thirty seconds of one teacher's time yet another consumes several minutes. In some classrooms the youngsters settle down in a few moments after recess, while in others the transition requires a half hour or more. Outdoor clothes can be put on without any particular agitation or only after a major battle. The artistic teacher is able to manage the class in such a way that these inevitable organizational details are accomplished as expeditiously as possible.[2]

The fourth of the special abilities, utilizing latent resources, relates primarily to teacher initiative. Resourcefulness is a habit as well as a skill. Many teachers who could be more enterprising are not mainly because they have limited aspirations. Those who are anxious to accomplish a good deal, and who are comfortable with a number of pedagogical chestnuts in their instructional fires, exploit possibilities wherever they can. The major barrier to resourcefulness is indifference: where goals are minimal and broad learning unvalued there is no need for industriousness.

Another obstacle to resourcefulness is the textbook. It is not that texts are undesirable, but rather that they too easily become a convenience that inhibits the imagination. For some teachers, the best textbook is the one which provides maximum structure and direction. Publishers take it as fact that the books most likely to enjoy high sales are those which are accompanied by comprehensive teaching guides, outlining a large number of instructional procedures. Obviously, there is nothing wrong with using texts and other prepared instructional materials nor with taking advantage of well-designed teaching activities. Total dependence on prefabricated devices, however, prevents the teacher from improvising, making subtle readjustments to the learning situation, and imbuing the lesson with stylistic color.

During the project, for example, a particularly creative teacher taught social studies without the use of any textbooks whatsoever. He worked extraordinarily hard, but student achievement was well above average. In the process, moreover, he developed a number of strategems for enlivening learning which became part of his permanent repertory. As an illustration, he began to devise assignments in which the students used newspapers as a source of current information. As in other aspects of human artistry, skillful performance lies not so much in relying on the tried and true, but in inventing what is needed.

In too many cases teaching has become a liturgy—a ritual where teachers are entirely dependent upon ready-to-use materials. It is remarkable, at times, how little extemporaneous activity goes on in instruction.

As with the other artistry themes, exercises were developed in an effort to heighten participant awareness. For example, teachers were presented with the following problem:

> Because of funding problems, it becomes necessary to close a school three weeks early. As a result, a teacher finds it essential to incorporate three units into one. Describe how you would integrate the following fifth-grade units:
>
> A. A social studies unit on the pilgrims
> B. A unit on writing topical outlines
> C. A math unit on time

Artistic teachers responded generally as follows: "First, teach topical outlines—their purposes and format. Second, have the students read the section of the text on pilgrims, and make a topical outline. Third, ask the students to calculate, from information given, the number of days and months it took groups, in different places, to cross the Atlantic."

In a second type of exercise, the emphasis was on choosing expedient procedures:

EFFICIENT ARTHMETIC INSTRUCTION

> Which of the following would be the most expedient way of teaching arithmetic to first-grade students?
> 1. Using pretests, prepared activities, and post-tests, have the children work individually.
> 2. Set up learning centers where all children work on the same arithmetic skills using manipulative materials: puzzles,

worksheets, games, and so on.
3. Divide the children into three groups, using separate tables, and ask each group to work on a specific objective.
4. Group the children according to ability and work with one group at a time.
5. Teach the entire class at once, using manipulative materials.
6. Teach the entire class at once, without the use of manipulative materials.

Although there were minor deviations, the most expedient approach, according to strong teachers, is 5, 2, 4, 3, 6, 1.

In a third kind of exercise, the intention was to highlight the importance of organizing the steps of a procedure in a sensible order:

TEACHING CHILDREN TO INFER

In teaching children to make inferences, what sequence—in the following five steps—would be the most efficient?
1. Ask the students a leading question.
2. Ask the students to make an inferential conclusion.
3. Ask the students to find the key words.
4. Ask the students to find the main idea.
5. Ask the students to read the sentence.

Here again, there were slight variations, but the more artistic teachers generally preferred something like 5, 3, 4, 1, 2.

As the artistry program progressed, I became more and more convinced that classrooms and lessons often suffer from over-simplicity, excessive plainness, and a lack of connectedness with life outside the classroom. As I thought about the special talents of expeditious teachers, I realized that all four elements—logical linkages, efficient procedures, circumvented impediments, and latent resources—together form an approach which might be called "collateral teaching."

Collateral teaching occurs when a primary teaching objective and one or more secondary objectives are attacked simultaneous-ly. Primary objectives usually involve skills or concepts inherent in the subject: paragraph structure, for example, or calculating loan interest. Secondary goals, in contrast, tend to deal with related learning: synthesizing ideas, avoiding distractions, or developing confidence. Primary objectives are built into the cur-riculum. Secondary ones, in most cases, are added on by the teacher. *"Take advantage of opportunities to clarify ideas and reinforce concepts"* became a commonplace piece of advice during the last stages of the experiment. Student understanding is not always immediate and learning must be hammered home again and again. Chance occurrences, furthermore, often provide perfect moments for reinforcement: situations where an idea can be seen, not as an abstraction, but as a concrete illustration. When these "ripe moments" are exploited, comprehension can improve greatly.

Collateral teaching separates the ordinary from the master teacher. The conventional instructor plods through the required content without regard for the additional possibilities inherent in the learning situation. The best teachers, on the other hand, engage in multiple pursuits. While supervising a seat assignment involving graphs, an expert teacher will warn one student about the pitfalls of haste, remind the class about a formula studied several weeks earlier, and explain, on the spur of the moment, the issues underlying nuclear energy. Those who use collateral teaching are sensitive to the vast potential in teaching and able to keep multiple aims in mind. They seem to have a fondness for complexity, or—put the other way—an impatience with simplicity. They like, in short, to work on a number of things at once.

Some use collateral teaching as a motivational stimulus. By tantalizing their students with a new skill that can be acquired, or a larger idea that can be thought about, or even an interesting riddle that can be answered, they dramatize the limitless bounds of learning. A few also use collateral activities as bait: "If you get a little better at reading you can find out what the sports writers are saying about Reggie Jackson!"

Many theorists contend that it is best to attack instructional objectives as straightforwardly as possible. For example, if a teacher is interested in improving arithmetic skills, it is better to use number drills than to assign word problems dealing with, say, family budgets. It should be pointed out, in addition, that there is a difference between teaching two substantive objectives directly—arithmetic skills and verb form—through collateral procedures and teaching through indirect methods that deal with the primary objective in roundabout fashion. Collateral teaching—working toward multiple objectives—highlights the interconnections between parallel aims, all of which are dealt with directly. Circular teaching, in contrast, deals with a single objective tangentially, incorporating ideas that are obliquely related. In a unit on foreign trade, the object may be to explain the principle of balance between income and expenditure. The teacher might describe a situation in which a nation has serious economic problems because its imports exceed its exports. In helping the class grasp the principle, however, she may show the students a sequence of analytical steps—a collateral addition—which illuminate a problem in balance of trade, and, at the same time, improve deductive reasoning.

Collateral teaching can also stem from a sense of urgency—from what might be called "pedagogical greed," an avaricious desire to teach as much as possible. More than once, I have been struck by the parallel between master teachers, expert mechanics, and those who are skilled in the kitchen. One cook washes the vegetables, then melts the butter, then seasons the roast—proceeding from task to task, a single step at a time. Another, somehow, does all three at once. The mediocre mechanic drains the engine oil, idly watching the liquid drip into a container. The expert one turns his attention elsewhere, lubricating one part and adjusting two others, before the draining is finished.

Their penchant for Promethean ambitions may be driven by ego, competitiveness, and dedication. Mainly, however, it is a declaration of personal efficacy. The finest teachers have a compelling urge to achieve something worthwhile. Because they have many pedagogical fish to fry, collateral teaching is, for them, indispensable; without it, they would be reduced to a pedestrian pace and cover but half the possible ground. They may work a little harder than their more middling colleagues, yet they seem less tired at day's end. The secret, perhaps, lies in the revitalization that comes from achievement.

Teachers who engage in collateral teaching share a common aversion to lost chance and wasted opportunity; they have little patience with aimless activity and inertia because they have a full agenda and want to accomplish as much as possible. They may, at times, seem to wander aimlessly, but observed more closely, the logic and order of their method becomes apparent. Teaching about government in the eighteenth century, they digress now and then to interesting tidbits on the food, dress, and cultural mores of the time. They work first with one thread and then another, but the fabric they are weaving always remains in mind.

Use temporary digressions, on related topics, to enrich lessons, stimulate interests, and increase pace. Digression, some would contend, diverts students from the main objective. Many artist teachers, however, reason differently. Meaningful additions of provocative ideas help to sustain student concentration, point up significance, enlarge meaning, and deepen learning.

Lest it be misconstrued, collateral teaching does not violate the principles of good methodology. Learners are not permitted to go their own way; instead, their attention is directed by the teacher's specific intention. Although a lesson may be interrupted briefly to address a secondary goal, the primary objective is not slighted. Through the review of previously learned material and the incorporation of auxiliary ideas, the substantive content is increased rather than decreased. The teacher's control over the classroom is tighter, not looser, since it is imperative that temporary deviations, or an impromptu appendage, be followed by return to the central purpose. The teacher must have a more exact understanding of the students' learning needs, as well as a more comprehensive grasp of the subject matter.

Because the teacher seeks to compress additional learning into the scheduled lesson, time must be used with greater efficiency. And, as a consequence of the quickened tempo, the teacher's directions should be more specific than usual. The connections must be apparent between the central and related ideas. A drill may be interspersed with a question about human morality; laughter touched off by a foolish answer to a question can lead to a short discussion on the effect of riducule, or the historical occasions when a seemingly silly idea later proved to have great merit; a child's inquiry as to "whether neatness counts" may lead to a capsule consideration of aesthetics. Collateral teaching comes from the teacher's aggressive efforts to broaden student learning and to take advantage of opportunities that are unnoticed or ignored by less able practitioners.

Two precautions are in order. First, there is a vast difference between the disciplined use of collateral techniques and teaching which is fragmented. Every digression must have a purpose. The prattling teacher who surfeits students with excessive, pointless verbiage, the wandering teacher who moves from topic to topic for no particular reason, and the disjointed teacher who simply goes in too many directions at once all produce havoc. Such teaching is ineffective and does not result in collateral teaching. Second, there are times when collateral teaching is entirely inappropriate. Some classes, for example, are disturbed by even minor deviations and it is then better to stay with the basic target. Further, when the primary objective is complicated and not easily grasped, secondary pursuits are best avoided. Finally, when children are too excited, or too fatigued, the teaching must remain simple and direct.

However, children are energized by collateral teaching. Conditioned through long experience to adjust their efforts to a teacher's gait, they give only what is asked. In a lethargic classroom, they resignedly inch along, doing the assigned chores. In a stimulating environment, however, they are caught up in the activity and adapt themselves to increased intensity.

Chatting with a nine-year-old girl, one afternoon, I casually asked how school was going. "Terrific!" she replied. "I've almost finished my science project; my reading rate is up three points; and I can do folk dances from four different countries!" Collateral teaching is expedient because it makes use of complementarity—the process wherein one thing supplements, and is supplemented by, another. An improved vocabulary makes for better writing, and better writing makes for greater interest in ideas. Having learned to appreciate the qualities of good prose, the student may read the history text with greater interest. Through collateral teaching students can connect ideas and experiences to enhance understanding.

Sandra Gregory hates the obligatory teaching of national holidays. She knows that some observance of Christmas, Easter, Memorial Day, and other holidays is desirable, but she dislikes taking time from her dominant love: the passionate pursuit of better grammar and rhetoric.

One year, not yet prepared with a Thanksgiving activity and in the midst of a unit on letter writing, she was captured by an imaginative notion. It dawned upon her, while musing over various possibilities, that she might ask the class to write a letter of thanks to a city official, expressing appreciation for his or her contribution to the community's welfare.

A city directory was easily procured, and each student selected an official. One chose the mayor; another, the chief of police; and a third, the supervisor of the animal shelter. In short order, every child had a correspondent and drafted a personal letter. The teacher checked the drafts for spelling and punctuation, final copies were made, and the letters mailed.

No more was thought about the matter until one day the student who had written the chief of police received an answer. In due course, most of the other students also received responses. Since the students had used school envelopes, the city officials sent their responses to the principal, asking that their letters be given to the students. Many of them, in addition, attached a note to the principal, commending the school for its thoughtful gesture. The teacher's stock, needless to say, rose considerably.

What is it, one might ask, that enables artist teachers to use collateral teaching expediently? Three things, in particular, seem to have a bearing:

First, these teachers invariably are guided by intense personal beliefs. Unwillingly to embrace secondhand values, they have strong convictions about what youngsters should learn. Some, for example, place heavy store upon resilience: they want their students to persist in the face of temporary failure. Others are hooked on writing skills: they value clarity of expression. Still others prize broad knowledge: their classrooms are sprinkled with references to Bach's twenty children, laser technology, and a new world record in the high jump. Each, however, is motivated by a powerful conception of what teaching should do, and gives free rein to inner impulse. Lessons are planned but there is always room for the unplanned. Because the teachers take personal pride in the accomplishments of their students, overcoming a learning problem is not only the child's victory, but their own as well.

Second, artist teachers are adept at rapid changeovers. They move from one thing to another with ease, effortlessly redirecting student concentration. An admonishment about split infinitives may be sandwiched in the middle of a social studies discussion; an explanation of group sanctions may emerge during the money collection for the field trip; and in the midst of the geography lesson the teacher may suddenly ask why different cultures share similar aspirations. Students adapt quickly to these intermittent digressions. The rudder that keeps them on course—despite frequent side excursions—is the teacher's ability to return to the central point. Collateral teaching, through expedient organization, enables a teacher to work toward several ends and to accomplish more in the same amount of time.

Third, artist teachers have something akin to "multiple vision." They are able to keep a number of objectives in mind, seemingly at all times. They remember that one child lacks confidence and another is erratic. They expect their students to recite the pledge to the flag, but also to know what "liberty and justice for all" implies. They are interested not only in good test scores, but in behaviors and growth not measured by tests.

Collateral teaching is a way of enlarging learning: To capitalize on its value teachers must work with a larger blueprint and function with greater expediency. They must cultivate spontaneity, rely more on intuitive impulse so that the chance for something extra can be seized, and use devices which facilitate quick "attentional shifts" so as to engineer a convenient departure from, and return to, the essential goal.

RECAPITULATION

Artist teachers operate with exceptional expediency by (a) using procedures which require minimum expenditures of energy and time, (b) determining, beforehand, what is most likely to work, (c) avoiding predictable obstacles, and (d) dealing with related objectives simultaneously. Their secret is that they choose effective methods—ones which accomplish things with dispatch—and use them skillfully.

Careful thought is given to means and ends. They approach even routine problems with an open mind, asking themselves "What do I want?" and "What is the best way to get it?" Over time, they may develop extraordinary resourcefulness in accomplishing tasks quicker and better.

Expediency also improves when the teacher is able to shift from activity to activity without an undue loss of motion, when there is a concentrated effort to eliminate redundant behavior and unnecessary steps; and when the teacher constantly fights student inertia. Some days, for example, we take forty minutes to get dressed. But when time is of the essence and there is an early plane to catch, we may manage it in ten. Artist teachers keep their students going, allowing as much time for a task as is really needed, but not more.

Lastly, expediency is extended by "pedagogical greed"—the profound desire to teach as much as possible. Great teachers keep a number of aims in mind, and frequently "add on," squeezing a bit extra into the agenda. They sense when collateral teaching is appropriate or inappropriate. And—to repeat an earlier admonition—they pursue their own special list of educational objectives.

SOME ISSUES

1. What signs indicate when collateral teaching is desirable?
2. Can skill in predicting the probable success of a learning activity be easily acquired?
3. How is resourcefulness best developed?

TIPS ON TEACHING AND LEARNING

The following section presents a series of tips on teaching that have been extracted from the professional literature. They were used with the teachers in the experiments to stimulate thought. Each tip is followed by a list of recommended readings that were also made available to the teachers. They set forth the pedagogical principles that underlie our conception of good methods. They make abundant sense and confirm what experienced practitioners have long assumed. Yet, there are highly skilled teachers who, at one time or another, violate all of the recommendations. Thus, the suggestions, while useful, are less than an adequate formula for excellence in teaching. Excellence, as I will try to argue later, depends not only upon the choice of sensible methods, but also upon the deftness with which the procedures are used.

Reproduced below is one of the "handouts" dealing with the research on teaching that was given to the teachers during the experiment. All of the research, of course, was not included in the handout, but the concepts provide a sampling of the scholarly theories made available to the participants.

1. *Using Time.* A considerable body of research confirms the importance of providing sufficient time for learning. Generally speaking, student achievement is tied to the amount of time spent on an objective. The time must be used efficiently, however, and not be consumed by peripheral matters such as passing out materials, scolding an inattentive student, and so on. Research also shows that intensity has an effect on learning. A shorter period of time, in which the teaching and learning are potent, tends to yield better results than a longer period in which concentration is likely to waver. Each situation is different and there are no binding rules. The teacher has to decide when an activity is no longer productive. The efficient use of time depends on good organization, effective classroom management, sensible choice of materials, and emphasis on priorities. The wise thing, then, is to budget the right amount of time for each important goal and arrange it so that time is used as economically as possible and students' attention does not wander.

Berliner, David C. "Tempus Educare." In Penelope L. Peterson and Herber J. Walbert (eds.), *Research on Teaching.* Berkelely, California: McCutchan Publishing Co., 1979.

Bloom, B. S. "Time and Learning." *American Psychologist* 29 (1974): 682–688.

Carroll, J. B. "A Model for School Learning." *Teachers College Record* 64 (1963): 723–733.

Stallings, J. A., and D. H. Kaskowitz. *Follow-Through Classroom Observation Evaluation 1972–73.* Menlo Park, California: Stanford Research Institute, 1974.

Wiley, D. E., and A. Harnischfeger. "Explosion of a Myth: Quantity of Schooling and Exposure to Instruction, Major Educational Vehicles." *Educational Researcher* (1974): pp. 7–12.

2. *Grouping.* Academic progress seems to be affected by the ways in which students are grouped. Learning is impeded when a child spends even a relatively small period of time on an inappropriate endeavor. Various devices can be used to improve judgments regarding student assignments and group placements. Test scores and habitual error patterns, for example, often

provide helpful clues. In addition, short conversations with students regarding difficulties, observation of classroom behavior, and intuitive hunches as to ways to motivate particular individuals can also aid in determining the best placement. The research seems to indicate, moreover, that placements based upon a combination of different criteria are far superior to those based upon a single indicator, because they allow the teacher to consider the child's interests, learning characteristics, and developmental level.

It is also important to regroup students frequently. Long-term assignment to one group, or to the same project, is likely to increase boredom and cause the loss of a feeling of progress. In contrast, when continual assessment is used as a basis for periodically regrouping or reassigning students, a sense of momentum develops. It is desirable, therefore, to carry out recurrent evaluations and to use the results in redirecting the child's efforts. Repeated checking for improvement, through a variety of procedures, enables the teacher to make better decisions about student placement.

Cooley, W. W., and G. Leinhardt. *Design for the Individualized Instruction Study: A Study of the Effectiveness of Individualized Instruction in the Teaching of Reading and Mathematics in Compensatory Education Programs.* Pittsburgh: Learning Research and Development Center, 1975.

3. *Discipline.* Controlling children's behavior, while it does not directly improve learning, does prevent excessive discipline problems from interfering with learning. Successful teachers use an almost endless variety of techniques to restrict misbehavior, reduce rule infractions, and sustain pupil effort.

In most cases, teacher control is more successful when there are clear rules regarding acceptable conduct; when such rules are kept to an essential minimum; when students understand the penalties which will be imposed if they are violated; when the teacher is impartial and consistent in assessing penalties. Good classroom control also keeps confusion and distraction to a minimum. Researchers have found that disruptive behavior is minimized, and student attentiveness maximized, when teachers use systematic procedures in their classroom management. Responding to rule violations in routine, expected ways gives students a sense of stability.

Effective control requires several other skills. For one, the teacher must be able to anticipate and deal with potential problems before they get out of hand. For example, a student having finished an assignment may invent some mischief while others are finishing, or an argument may develop between two children sharing a map. Another student—about to be overcome by frustration—may begin to look for diversion. Teachers who take the trouble to know their students can anticipate by sensing the early signs. Second, the teacher must be able to shift from activity to activity without undue agitation. Valuable time can be lost and incentive dissipated when such transitions are clumsy. Third, teachers must be able to work with a small group or an individual without losing contact with the rest of the class.

Classroom mood is influenced but not entirely determined by the teacher's management procedures. In classrooms with a good emotional tone, some teachers allow the students a reasonable amount of freedom, while others are more tightly constrained. Similarly, in those with a poor emotional tone, the structure is sometimes loose, and sometimes tight. In short, a teacher can be strict without resorting to sarcasm, or permissive, without allowing the students to run wild. An absence of control does not make students happier, just as the enforcement of sensible rules does not destory their contentment.

Bidwell, C. "The Social Psychology of Teaching." In R. M. W. Travers (ed.), *Second Handbook of Research on Teaching*. Chicago: Rand McNally, 1973.

Kounin, J. S. *Discipline and Group Management in Classrooms*. New York: Holt, Rinehart and Winston, 1970.

Evertson, C. M., and J. E. Brophy. *High-Inference Behavioral Ratings as Correlates of Teaching Effectiveness*. Austin: University of Texas, Research and Development Center for Teacher Education, 1973.

Soar, Robert S., and Ruth M. Soar. "Classroom Behavior, Pupil Characteristics, and Pupil Growth for the School Year and for the Summer." *JSAS Catalogue of Selected Documents in Psychology* 5 (1975): 200 (MS. No. 873).

4. *Organizing Instruction.* In all likelihood, native ability has more to do with student achievement than anything else. However, since teachers cannot alter natural endowment, the important consideration becomes: what can teachers do in organizing instruction to increase learning?

Among other things, researchers believe that it is of great importance to work toward specific objectives. Without clear goals, learning achievement is reduced. It is equally important to approach these goals through carefully planned steps. Wherever possible, the learning activities should be arranged in the best possible sequential order. There are, unfortunately, few principles to aid teachers in determining an ideal sequence, and thus a certain amount of trial and error is necessary.

Frequent interim evaluations also appear to be helpful. Tests can be given in a variety of ways, so long as they give some indication of student progress and clues as to what would further facilitate learning. In addition, it is essential that learners receive systematic feedback. Students learn more efficiently when they know not only how well they are doing, but also where their major difficulties lie.

There is reason to believe, moreover, that there often is a disparity between the instructional goals, the content used, and the achievement tests. Particularly in the case of standardized tests, designed for general use, students may be taught material that differs from that on which they will be tested. Teachers should ensure that their materials are congruent with the designated instructional goals, and that the content coincides with the testing measures that will be given. It also helps to familiarize students with the different kinds of test items which may be used. If the student has not had experience with the kinds of testing procedures that are employed, the achievement scores may be deceptively low.

While the research suggests that goals, content, and testing must be consistent, other steps are also advantageous. Therefore, teachers are well advised to use personal judgment and draw upon their own experience in organizing instruction. John B. Carroll, one of the most distinguished theorists, has even suggested that a commonsense approach to teaching helps fill in the gaps in the research findings.

Carroll, John B. "Promoting Language Skills: The Role of Instruction." In David Klahr (ed.), *Cognition and Instruction*. Hillsdale, New Jersey: Lawrence Erlbaum Associates, 1976.

Cooley, W. W., and G. Leinhardt. *The Application of a Model for Investigating Classroom Processes*. Pittsburgh: University of Pittsburgh, Learning Research and Development Center, 1975.

Doyle, W. "Classroom Tasks and Student Abilities." In P. L. Peterson and H. J. Walberg (eds.), *Conceptions of Teaching*. Berkeley, California: McCutchan, 1979.

Rosenshine, B. "Classroom Instruction." In N. L. Gage (ed.), *The Psychology of Teaching Methods. Seventy-fifth Yearbook of the National Society for the Study of Education, Part 1*. Chicago: University of Chicago Press, 1976.

5. *Teaching Strategies.* Some of the most thoughtful studies on teaching have been done by Donald Medley. He believes that the most useful measure of a teacher's effectiveness is the amount of content students learn in a given period of time. Teacher ratings, however, should make due allowance for pupil ability and other conditions over which teachers have no control. Although much of his research has been done with disadvantaged children, the conclusions may be equally applicable to all students.

Medley also acknowledges that stuffing facts into children, which they can remember long enough to pass a test, is not the central purpose of teaching. Education should produce permanent changes in behavior, instill good attitudes and values, and develop productivity and self-reliance. The ultimate goal is to make the student a happy, useful member of society. Hence, even though children are taught a great deal of subject matter which they promptly forget, the content should be viewed as a vehicle for accomplishing the larger goals.

Effective teaching strategies result in classrooms which are systematic and psychologically secure. The strategies should be chosen with a view to minimizing disruptive behavior, so that little of the teacher's time is devoted to discipline and most of it can be spent on academic learning. The teaching strategies should maximize student concentration. As a general rule, it is easier to maintain concentration and monitor individual student progress when the entire class works on the same activity. In such cases guidance and direction can be provided more efficiently, distractions are reduced, and student difficulties can be detected and remedied more readily.

The most successful teachers, moreover, guard against an excessive number of student questions and keep their answers short. This suggests that extensive time devoted to answering student questions may not materially improve learning.

Surprisingly, teachers who ask their students short, direct

questions—requiring specific answers—seem to get better results than those who raise more complicated issues, requiring speculative thought. Nonetheless, incisive probing, aimed at the key points, is most beneficial.

Medley, Donald M. *Teacher Competence and Teacher Effectiveness*. Washington, D. C.: American Association of Colleges for Teacher Education, 1977.

6. *Reinforcement*. Learning improves when the teacher provides a variety of psychological supports such as encouragement, praise for good work, and reassurance. Teachers who take a limited responsibility for the success of their students are not inclined to provide such supports. Other teachers who feel obligated to inspire learning and are genuinely gratified when a child achieves avoid flattery and false commendation but are quick to point out when authentic progress has taken place. They seem, in addition, to have an expectation that everyone *will* learn.

In the area of fundamental skills, amount and rate of learning increase when the assignments are based upon small, steady increments. As Madeline Hunter has ably demonstrated, pupils should be given considerable opportunity for repeated practice and correction of mistakes; when success occurs, the teacher should make certain that the child takes satisfaction in the accomplishment.

Psychological reinforcement is also promoted by regularity and routine. When materials are distributed and collected in the same way each day, customary procedures followed for such activities as asking questions and sharpening pencils, and rule infractions dealt with in a fair and consistent manner, students are more secure and able to work more diligently. With an efficient classroom routine, less teacher time is required for controlling disruptions. As success is reinforced, students gradually become more confident, more able to function by themselves, and more inclined to expect future success.

Bossert, Steven T. ''Tasks, Group Management, and Teacher Control Behavior: A Study of Classroom Organization and Teacher Style.'' *School Review* 85 (1977).

Brophy, Jere E., and Carolyn M. Evertson. *Learning from Teaching: A De-*

velopmental Perspective. Boston: Allyn and Bacon, 1976.

Good, Thomas L., and Douglas Grouws. "Teaching Effects: A Process-product Study in a Fourth Grade Mathematics Classroom." *Journal of Teacher Education*, May–June, 1977.

Hunter, Madeline. *Rx for Improved Instruction*. El Segundo, Calif.: TIP Publications, 1976.

Mehan, Hugh. "Accomplishing Classroom Lessons." In Aaron V. Cicourel et al. (eds.), *Language Use and School Performance*. New York: Academic Press, 1974.

Kounin, J. A. *Discipline and Group Management in Classrooms*. New York: Holt, Rinehart and Winston, 1970.

In the spring of 1982, when I was finishing this manuscript, I noticed an article in the April *Phi Delta Kappan*. In an essay entitled "Successful Teaching Strategies for the Inner-City Child," Jere Brophy summarized matters thus: "Effective instruction in the basic skills involves determination to teach these skills thoroughly, careful allocation of classroom time to this purpose, organization and management of the classroom to involve students in academic activities, programming for brisk curriculum pacing and easy success, active instruction and supervision, and teaching to mastery."

The research on pedagogy describes the competencies and characteristics of skillful teachers. It tells us *what* should be done, but not *how* it should be done. One can motivate a child, for example, through reward or threat, just as student attention can be captured through nagging or intrigue. The research on artistry, in contrast, tells us a bit more about the "how." It sheds light on stylistic alternatives and clarifies, somewhat, the effects of compassion, flamboyance, spontaneity, and imagination.

Pedagogy involves both art and science in teaching because neither, by itself, is sufficient. An exciting personality is a great asset, but there must also be form. Similarly, a good knowledge of subject and method is of little avail when the teaching is wearisome and lackluster. The interdependence of the two is made plain when we recognize that a weakness on one side can often be offset by a strength on the other.

School administrators easily distinguish between good and bad teaching. If asked to compare two faculty members, they can readily observe that Smith is better than Jones, or the reverse. They may even be able to describe the particular qualities which made one superior to the other. No sensible administrator, however, believes that all good teachers exhibit the same characteristics. In short, there are few universals in pedagogy. A routine that is significant for one teacher may be merely an encumbrance of procedure for another. The mark of worth lies not in method but in outcome.

The impact of a teacher on a child is always subject to circumstance. Even the most adept teachers encounter students, now and then, with whom they are unsuccessful. But the opposite can also be true. An instructor who borders upon the incompetent can, upon occasion, make a profound contribution to a given child. During my conversation with faculties, when I was trying to grasp the nebulous nature of artistry, I frequently would ask: "Did you ever have a great teacher? What traits produced greatness?" In one memorable instance, an exceedingly bright young man said thoughtfully, "He was an extremely bad teacher, but he was marvelous for me!" Puzzled, I asked for a further explanation.

"It was in the small town where I grew up," he said. "The teacher taught junior high science. A tragic man, really. He was a manic-depressive and an alcoholic. He deserted his wife and four kids when the eldest child was twelve. There were twenty-four students in our science class, but he totally ignored twenty of them, and spent all of his time with four of us—his favorites."

"What made him great?" I asked.

"He taught me to think for myself, and he genuinely cared about what I did with my mind."

It is for these reasons that the pedagogical "tips" on teaching, while constructive and informative, are far from absolute. Many gifted teachers disregard them, from time to time, when the situation requires a temporary deviation from normal practice.

The value of *pedagogical intelligence*—the accumulation of experience, insight, and professional cunning—has not been adequately advertised. Difficulties frequently arise in the classroom for which there are no routine answers. All teachers try, if only now and then, to avoid a concession to mediocrity and find a unique solution; in so doing, they call upon their pedagogical intelligence to devise a maneuver which may work. Describing this process is worrisome, because the deeper rhythms of the mind are easily misunderstood. Nonetheless, what they do, I suspect, is pose and resolve conjectural problems for themselves.

Consider, as an example, a teacher who wishes to teach her students how to classify flowers. She may ask herself:

1. How are flowers classified?
2. What must one *know* in order to classify flowers?
3. How can this knowledge most easily be acquired?
4. How can I best facilitate such acquisition?
5. What signs will tell me when the necessary knowledge has been acquired?
6. What can be done to make the acquisition of learning interesting?

In pondering these questions the teacher works from objective, to means, to verification. The process results in what we call "a method." Note, however, that the method can be either good or bad *and* it may be used artfully or artlessly.

Schematically, the process can be illustrated as follows:

Elements in Teaching

Knowledge of Topic	Method	Quality
1. Facts	6. Learning Principles	10. Creativity
2. Laws	7. Instructional Principles	11. Spontaneity
3. Concepts	8. Stylistic Preferences	12. Perceptivity
4. Principles	9. Situational Adaptations	13. Decision Making
5. Generalizations		

One could, obviously, extend the number of elements beyond the thirteen listed above. The illustration, however, suffices to indicate that effective teachers must have (1) a good knowledge of the subject matter they teach, (2) an understanding of the ways humans learn, (3) a familiarity with good instructional procedure, (4) a personalized approach to teaching, (5) an ability to adjust their procedures to the particular situation, and (6) a desire and aptitude for skillful performance.

While I was working with schools, I often asked principals and superintendents which of these factors they considered most important. In nine cases out of ten, after acknowledging that the knowledge components were crucial, they placed the heaviest emphasis upon numbers ten to thirteen. They had learned, from long experience, that teachers vary considerably in their approach, and that good results can be obtained in different ways. They also knew, from years of teacher-watching, that the factors relating to excellence and artistry were sufficiently powerful that

Teacher Profiles

Knowledge of Subject	Knowledge of Learning Principles	Knowledge of Teaching Principles	Knowledge of Teaching Methods	Effective Style	Artistic Qualities
A strong	moderate	weak	moderate	moderate	moderate
B strong	weak	moderate	weak	strong	strong
C strong	strong	strong	strong	weak	weak

they counterbalanced weaknesses elsewhere. In the profiles of the three teachers above, A, B, and C, it is likely that all three would obtain somewhat similar results, simply because their strengths and weaknesses tend to equalize one another.

To further compound the complexity, we must also reckon with the learner's ability and will. Bright children who have a strong urge to learn invariably master a subject even when their teaching is poor. There is, in sum, a law of compensating forces that underscores teaching and learning. Because a great many variables are involved, the overall importance of each is somewhat neutralized. It may well be, consequently, that we have greatly exaggerated the importance of method and standard procedure. Methodology, after all, is no more than an extension of what we call sensible action, or elementary logic. Put bluntly, what works, works.

The idea of compensating forces deserves, perhaps, further elaboration. The bright college-bound youngster, preparing for his entrance examinations, will learn calculus even if it is badly taught. His own incentive will repair the defects of poor pedagogy. Other students, fortunate enough to receive good teaching, will also learn, but it is unlikely that their instruction will be uniform. There are rule followers and rule breakers in teaching. Both succeed if the *gestalt* is right. Compensating forces will nullify a deficit in one place and an excess in another. When the learning falters, and a good teacher perceives that he/she has erred in judgment, he/she immediately takes corrective steps. A beguiling teaching style can make up for a weak method, and powerful enthusiasm can counter liabilities stemming from imprecise techniques. It is the aggregate effect that matters.

Teachers who, through self-education, have developed their pedagogical intelligence, make use of compensating forces. Pedagogical intelligence is instructional wisdom, ''child sense,'' a special kind of classroom sagacity bred out of long experience that allows teachers to be resourceful and enterprising. It is the ability to be flexible in reaching a goal. To the discerning, pedagogical intelligence is most apparent in the capacity of artist teachers to overcome obstacles.

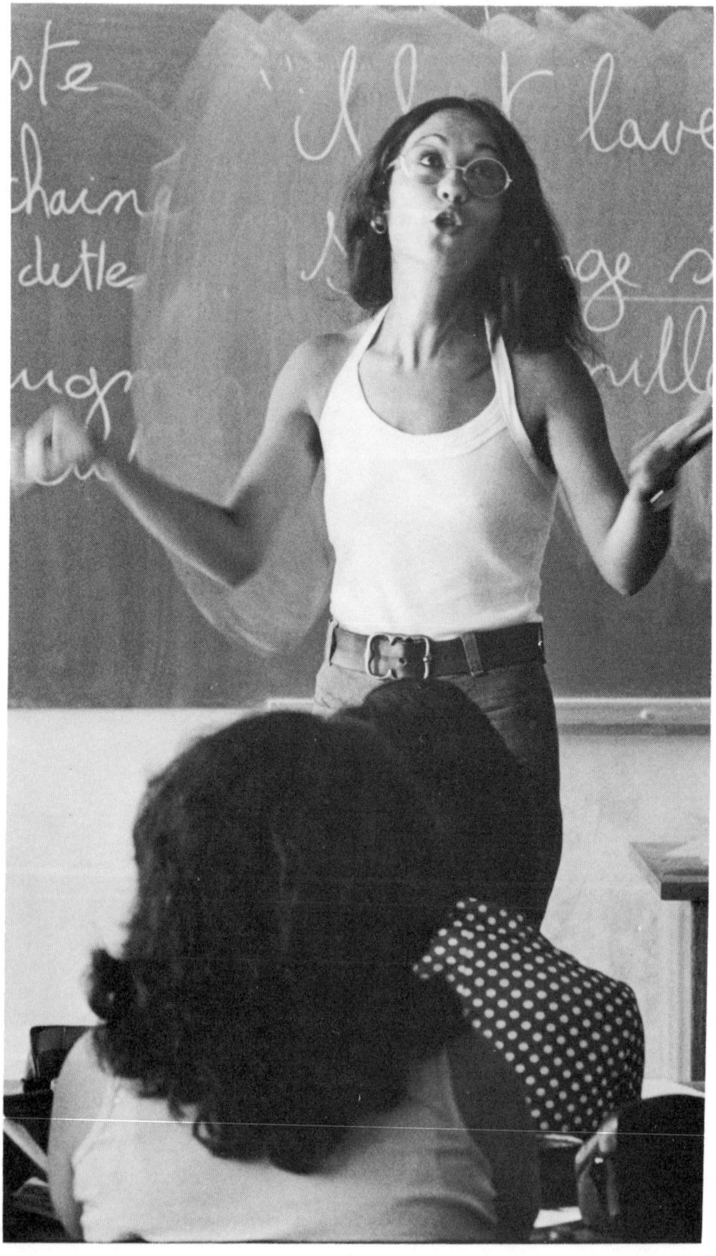

PART TWO

Teaching As Theater

Every work of art has one indispensable mark . . . the centre of it is simple, however much the fulfillment may be complicated.

G. K. Chesterton
''The Queer Feet''

7

THE EXPERIMENT

The conviction that artistic teaching involves far more than using sensible procedures led to a series of informal experiments which I carried out over the course of several years while teaching at the University of Illinois and Stanford University. The purpose of the experiments was to determine whether, through various maneuvers, the artistry of teachers could be heightened. Putting method and content temporarily aside, would it be possible to arrange learning experiences that enabled teachers to make their classrooms more exciting and appealing?

It was obvious that the participating teachers would have to meet several requirements. First, they would need an interest in becoming more artistic. Next, they would have to devise tactics for engendering greater student motivation. Third, the teachers would have to master a sense of timing; that is, to learn when each particular tactic was most appropriate. Fourth, they would need to acquire a "feel" for judicious balance, so as to prevent instruction from deteriorating into a game or amusement. And last, they would have to be persuaded to invest something extra in the way of effort because artist teachers must themselves be inspired.

The experiments—first at the University of Illinois, then at Stanford University, and ultimately in a number of school districts throughout the country—were based on several assumptions about the teaching-learning process. First, children need not hate school. Second, tedium is not essential to learning. Third, boredom is neither unavoidable nor inevitable. And fourth, even the dullest of subjects can be taught in a way that intrigues the learner. Although scholarship involves hard work, strenuous effort can, in its own way, be rewarding. Beyond these four there was the basic assumption that teaching is an art form, and that many classroom problems which haunt and vex teachers might be circumvented through imaginative instruction.

Although these notions may seem simple-minded they provided a starting point. Since the anatomy of artistry is fuzzy, and little is known about the mechanics through which great teachers develop their greatness, these assumptions served to woo the participants into exploring the boundaries of their talent.

The experiment consisted of an effort to enhance teaching virtuosity through deliberate creative invention. Reversing customary training arrangements where ready-made devices are modeled, the strategy was to stimulate a do-it-yourself attitude. I wanted to find out whether teachers could become conscious of their own productive powers, could learn to exploit the situational factors that exist in every lesson and to create instruction that fit their own natural style. Since master practitioners vary in their methodology, we asked if it would be possible to fashion an approach that took maximum advantage of individual strengths. And, above all, could the elusive qualities associated with artistry be cultivated?

In essence, the experiments were an attempt to determine whether the professional self-education of teachers could increase artistry, particularly with respect to a more dramatic pedagogical style which capitalized on personal attributes. The invitation to participate was straightforward: I argued that teaching was a performing art and asked potential participants if they would be interested in experimenting with some motivational techniques used in theater. In my own mind I harbored other hopes as well. Working toward a more dramatic style might also deepen teachers' involvement, increase their work satisfaction, and help counteract professional disillusionment. Moreover, heartened by more enthusiastic students, teachers might come to recognize that unwitting conformity is counterproductive; they might, then, develop an instinctive hunch about the right things to do and display a keener interest in their students. In turn, this might prompt a wish to learn more about their students' private lives and inner thoughts. For it is only when the teacher accurately deciphers the mind of the child that the best teaching is possible. And, as much as anything else perhaps, I hoped that the experimental activities would result in greater professional ego, coupled with a corresponding pride in craft, and encourage teachers to communicate the particular appeal of their subjects and the general joys of learning.

The major purpose of the experiment was to determine, if I could, how gifted teachers increase student motivation, involvement, and concentration; how rigorous intellectual pursuit could be encompassed in teaching procedures that excited students a bit; whether teaching finesse could be acquired through practice; if there was, in fact, any real basis for presuming a common ground between teaching and theater; and whether teachers could devise instructional tactics which—in addition to jibing with their stylistic inclinations—also stirred the souls of their students.

Beyond these fundamental questions, there were several other quests about which I wanted to think further, some ancient riddles: Can teachers, working autonomously, perpetuate their own professional growth, or is it essential to have some sort of external coaching? Can every teacher learn, through trial and error, to function more effectively? What special capacities enable some to teach with exceptional distinction? What teaching characteristics are most closely associated with true artistry? And, in the same vein, would an effort to teach with high artistry increase the job satisfaction of teachers or, instead, produce excessive stress?

In addition, I wanted to consider some unanswered conundrums: which constructs from our knowledge of human psychology would be most useful in stimulating the inventive capabilities of teachers; what factors dull teachers' imaginations and cause them to use the same repetitive maneuvers again and again; and whether creative teaching is best inspired by example or by personal search.

I was equally curious about the effects of artistic teaching on learners: Would they learn more or less, exhibit greater interest in the teacher or the subject matter, develop a temporary or lasting interest in learning? Finally, in what seemed the most complicated of my objectives, I wanted to find out as much as I could about the ways in which artistic teaching evolves.

It was this last question, chiefly, which accounted for the experiment's longevity. All in all, the study went on for a little over four years. Some aspects fell into place relatively easily, and others were a good deal more problematic. The question of artistic invention serves as a case in point: Imaginative teachers sometimes bury their creativity out of the fear that an innovative tactic will anger their superiors. Once inventive courage is resurrected, however, and dormant potentialities awakened, all sorts of inspired strategies may emerge. Precisely how these come into being, nonetheless, often remains an enigma. Teachers themselves, in fact, are sometimes at a loss to explain the impulse which led them in the right direction.

Because of the experiment's informality, there was little rigid structure. Whenever opportunity occurred, I traveled here and there, explaining my aspirations to a school faculty and—if the bait was taken—attempted to sustain further interest by telephone and mail. Then, on subsequent visits, I talked with teachers and administrators, seeking answers to some of the riddles. For example, it was in Princeton, Ohio that I first became aware of the powerful inhibitions unleashed by the fear of failure. Many teachers would rather use timeworn methods—however prosaic and lackluster—than try something which might not work. And it was in Costa Mesa, California, that I first encountered a phenomenon which was to occur again and again: namely, a resistance to artistic experimentation—on the part of some secondary school teachers—because of their strong concern for the subject matter itself. Similarly, I was rejected by a district in upstate New York because the experiment lacked an organized set of materials; and—on the plus side of the ledger—in Maryland, four teachers from a rural school formed their own "artistry club" after their faculty declined my invitation to participate.

At the outset, I had no particular number of participants in mind. The teachers who participated in the experiments were recruited randomly. In the beginning, the majority were concentrated around Palo Alto, California, and Champaign, Illinois. During the four years of the experiment, as I fulfilled consulting assignments around the country I was able to reach faculties elsewhere until, ultimately, I had what could be considered a reasonable cross-section of the nation—three districts in California, two in Ohio, four in Pennsylvania, two in Texas, and soon one in Florida. Interest tended to be somewhat higher in suburban districts than in cities. In most instances, the involvement began with a district-sponsored inservice activity which later shifted to individual school faculties. At the peak of the investigation, I concentrated my attention on twenty selected schools, so as to study the effect of the talks to teachers, handouts, and other distributed materials. All told, I gathered some sort of data on roughly 350 teachers. This core group remained involved for varying lengths of time. Some terminated after a month or two and others, I have reason to believe, are still engaged in an effort to teach more artistically.

Participants were of all ages, with varying amounts of experience. Some teachers were in their first professional year, others in their thirtieth. A good many older teachers took part—some of whom, it might be added, eventually attained exceptional levels of artistry. While enthusiasm differed from individual to individual, there was no correlation with service years: a teacher with fifteen years of experience was just as likely to be interested—or uninterested—as one who had taught only a year or two.

Roughly sixty-five percent of the participants were women and thirty-five percent men, presumably because of the long-standing imbalance in the profession.

Usually, between fifty and ninety percent of a given faculty experimented with the exercise. The commitment of the principal was undoubtedly a key factor, at least in fostering initial teacher interest;[1] there was substantially less participation when the principal gave the experiment little attention. Similarly, on each faculty there were a few teachers who were status leaders, and their involvement or lack of involvement influenced others.

Although no statistical data were obtained, I had a pervasive feeling that the best of the teachers were the most interested. Many potential participants, for example, were alienated by the lack of a prescribed system; since the teachers were given little more than a speech on teaching as a performing art, a few models, and a bit of theoretical background. Although the absence of compulsory requirements and the privilege of dropping out at any point was reassuring, many teachers would have preferred more explicit direction.

The press of my other responsibilities made a considerable time lag between the recruitment of the first and last school inevitable. I therefore hoped that the success of these already engaged in the experiment would help in soliciting additional teachers. However, my speculations were wrong. Schools chose to participate or not participate for a variety of reasons, but the response of one school did not seem to influence another. In the beginning, my intent was to enlist an entire faculty, on the grounds that total participation would increase group solidarity. I found, however, that in a number of situations one or two individuals were unwilling or unable to devote time to the enterprise, and I simply went ahead without them.

The second major stage of the experiment, beginning at the onset of the third year, was marked by my decision to focus on the faculties from twenty selected schools. By reducing the number I was able to test specific improvement procedures. Several factors prompted this decision. For one thing, a fair amount of attrition occurred during the first two years. For another, with the passing of time I gradually formed some preliminary hypotheses about teaching artistry, and I wanted to test these conclusions in fresh situations. I was anxious to learn, for example, whether the distribution of background information, handouts, and suggestion sheets actually helped facilitate teachers' efforts at self-improvement. Those who began during the first stage, of course, were welcome to continue and, indeed, many did. With the new faculties, however, I was able to take advantage of lessons I had learned earlier. Thus, most of the convictions which appear in the Epilogue came out of a two-stage evolution.

The somewhat random involvement of teachers became more systematic in the second stage. In the usual case, I attended a faculty meeting and described the program, the conditions of participation, and the insights gleaned from the first stage. If the faculty agreed to participate, I then returned at a later point for a second meeting and suggested a plan of action. I urged the teachers to work at more artistic teaching at times when the situation seemed appropriate. I suggested they experiment either individually or in small groups, depending upon their preference.

An overview, describing the purpose of the experiment and examples of the four concepts described in Chapters 9–12 was distributed. I also arranged, during the first of the three orientation meetings which followed a faculty's decision to participate, some procedure for further communication. More often than not, the teachers were separated into small groups, with one individual serving as the group representative. In this way, through later telephone and letter contact with the representatives, I was able to follow a school's progress with reasonable ease.

Early in the second stage, while working with one of the selected faculties, I had a useful insight. I was preparing for a second orientation meeting at which I intended to answer questions, clarify misconceptions, and talk briefly about the principles of self-directed professional growth. Since I am an early riser—and inordinately fond of long, hot showers—I was in the bathtub of a New York hotel, pondering the best way to make the presentation. My major concern had to do with finding adequate time in which the teachers could plan their artistic endeavors. Those who teach live full lives, and experience had taught me that there are limits to the number of personal hours teachers can be expected to devote to professional pursuits. It dawned on me, suddenly, that if *I* could plan while showering, other teachers might just as easily utilize their own bathing time in similar fashion. Later in the day, at the orientation meeting, I pointed out that participation did not require the taking of tests, outside reading, or the preparing of papers. The one necessity, I added, was that each teacher would be expected to devote roughly twenty minutes of "bathtub time" a week to the experiment. Noting that bathing rituals are largely mechanical, irrespective of individual habit, I pointed out that the time spent in bathtubs can be used to think about whatever one wishes. All teacher planning connected with the experiment, therefore, could be carried out in this way. The teachers needed only to think about a lesson they intended to teach in the next few days, invent some new way of doing the teaching, and then test the invention at the intended time. Thus, to anticipate the themes of later chapters, any teacher could, periodically, fabricate a dramatic episode or staging device or devise some imaginative gambit for improving the classroom atmosphere. This proposition, surprisingly, was so well received that it became standard operating procedure.

As I worked with faculties during the orientation meetings, the nature of my task gradually became more clear. Once a group evidenced an interest in pursuing artistic performance and understood the critical distinction between selecting a method and using it with finesse, my role became predominantly one of facilitator and energizer. The important things were to build incentive, promote enthusiasm, and counter the anxieties associated with failure. Through trial and error, I eventually discovered that the best way to achieve these goals was through the sharing of artistic inventions, both successful and unsuccessful, among the teachers. Once they had developed sufficient rapport, inhibitions fell and they could freely describe what they had created and speculate about why it did or did not work. Like other professionals, pedagogues display considerable interest in the endeavors of their colleagues. The parading of battle scars, as much as anything else, helped sustain zeal.

Early in the beginning stage I kept a roster of individual participating teachers, mainly for communication purposes. Later, when I was working with the schools, it became easier to maintain contact through either a faculty representative or the principal. I tried to continue at least minimal interchange with the teachers who became involved during the first two years, initiating direct communication with a teacher when conversation with the building contact suggested it would be advisable. And I was able, in many instances, to revisit a school after the three orientation meetings. It was during these return visits that I sought, through observation and discussion, to get a better understanding of teaching artistry.

As a partial substitute for on-scene presence, I periodically mailed materials to the building representatives for distribution. Four mimeographed newsletters called "Tips on Teaching" were sent during the third and fourth years. These contained for the most part practical ideas extracted from the writings of other researchers; for example, Jacob Kounin's observations on "withitness," Benjamin Bloom's theories regarding "mastery learning"; Barak Rosenshire's findings on the effects of enthusiasm; and Jane Stalling's recommendations on reinforcement.[2] In addition, whenever I accumulated enough anecdotal material to do so, I mailed a loosely constructed memo describing successful teacher inventions and interesting developments in various participating schools. These memoranda were my only way of carrying on communication between schools.

Near the end, however, a bit of direct interaction began to occur. A faculty representative from one school, for example, might write or phone another representative to find out whether the teachers were having difficulties with the "acting" metaphor. Or a group of teachers from several schools would, on their own, arrange to exchange dramatic episodes. Although I knew that such communication transpired, it was impossible to keep any sort of precise record.

In the three "talks to teachers," my original intent was to present them personally in each school. I again discovered, regrettably, that I had underestimated time demands and schedule complications. I did manage, with a bit of juggling, to give at least one talk at each site. When it was impossible to get to the school, I sent each teacher a copy of the text through the faculty representative. My hunch is that while an animated presentation is generally more appealing than printed matter, the major ideas probably were conveyed with similar effectiveness.

The "talks" were an outgrowth of my increasing sophistication regarding artistry. From the very start I conversed with teachers, both individually and in groups, about extending professional competence. I also visited a great many classrooms. Sometimes these visits stemmed from an invitation and, in other situations, I asked if I might observe something which struck me as interesting. My reason for these visits was to enlarge my own understanding. Patterns eventually began to take shape: I reached the conclusion, for example, that the most artistic of teachers were rich in several particular talents, such as the ability to perceive and decode clues in student behaviors, an aptitude for intuitive decision making, and a capacity to adapt creatively. Accordingly, each of these attributes eventually became the topic of a "talk." In organizing the presentations, I collected current theory on the subject and applied it to the concept of artistic teaching.

It was interesting to observe the manner in which teachers gradually adapted to the tasks. At the outset of the experiments, there was, not surprisingly, some reluctance and some minor difficulties. Inventive problem solving was, for many, a relatively new experience, and a pervasive fear was that an invented device might not work. Creative behavior, moreover, is not without its stresses and tensions and in some cases teachers focused their energies on the wrong problems. Accustomed to following routines, people sometimes are thrown by the sudden need to find different procedures. In the resulting tension, they may confuse cause and effect. For example, one teacher erroneously assumed that class misbehavior stemmed from the students' dislike of the subject, which, in this instance, was social studies. She therefore attempted to devise a classroom game which would illustrate human adaptation to environments, as well as create greater learner interest. The game was invented, decorum improved briefly, and the unruliness then returned. In a random conversation with a child, she unexpectedly discovered that the class liked the study topics, but became restless because of the frequent repetition. In a subsequent effort at instructional design, she produced a series of individual projects which could be undertaken by students as soon as the classroom assignment was completed. Her difficulties with misconduct vanished.

In time, substantial progress beccame evident. The participants eventually developed psychological defenses against failure and came to accept periodic obstacles as an inevitable consequence of creative endeavor rather than as a personal weakness. Their creativity began to flow more easily, and they became increasingly perceptive about the kinds of learning problems worth attacking. The great advantage, in this regard, was that each teacher could, at will, experiment with his or her own class. Since the experiments occurred when schools were in session, a tactic could be contrived on a Saturday afternoon, tested on Monday, revised Monday night, and tried again, with a different group of students, on Tuesday.

As the teachers tried one device and then another, they developed, bit by bit, a feel for the kinds of things that worked best with particular classes. And, by degrees, they sharpened their conceptions about instruction. The continuous experimentation seemed to unravel some of the mysteries regarding success and failure in learning.

8

THE CLASSROOM AS THEATER

The classroom and the theater share a number of parallels. For the young, school—a major aspect of their lives—is itself a real-life drama. It exposes them to the full range of human feeling: excitement, tension, conflict, disillusionment, joy, and frustration. Tears and laughter, euphoria and despair, gaiety and sadness are as much a part of schooling as pencils and erasers. The educational drama results not only from the interpersonal counterpoint, but also from the ways instruction is organized and administered. Teachers must command attention, sustain concentration, overcome listlessness, and resurrect self-confidence. They do these things, quite often, by drawing upon the same psychological principles used by playwrights, stage directors, and actors.

Both school and drama, for example, are meant to be experienced directly. A play that is read, or the description of a missed session at school, may provide a sense of what transpired, but the real spirit of the events is lost. Much like theater audiences, students bring their own experience to the schoolroom and respond to the events in different ways. Teacher unfairness may remind one child of a hostile father, and another of the disillusionment experienced after an argument with a trusted friend.

The theater and the classroom must both assume previous knowledge. To understand a play, the audience should recognize from some sort of prior experience the implication of the plot and its attendant meanings. In much the same fashion, students must—through earlier learning—grasp the teacher's desire, and connect the teaching with what they already know. If, for one reason or another, these connections are not made, learning is thwarted—much as an audience, unable to understand a play's development, becomes frustrated. Student and playgoer both use their past frames of reference to interpret what is going on.

Classroom and theater create what Susanne Langer termed the "perpetual present moment."[1] Like riding a roller coaster, sitting in a dentist's chair, or walking through fresh snow, stage scenes and classroom happenings are grasped and internalized only as they are experienced. Whether a crisis in history is relived through a history book or a stage drama, it becomes a part of our memory bank. Each event becomes a new link in one's chain of life encounters. Some people can stand on a street corner for hours on end, observing one passerby after another, simply because each passing awakens different reactions and because each adds to the cumulative total of sensory impression. Instant by instant, the unfolding drama, whether in a classroom or a playhouse, brings fresh adventure.

Acting and teaching also share a dependence upon spontaneity. Every performance of an opera or musical comedy is unique, just as classrooms are never mirror images of one another. The classroom itself, the assignments, and the instructional methods may be the same, but each class nonetheless takes its own special form. Professors who have taught the same course for thirty years to sixty different classes are likely to find that each was distinct: one class required an extra hour or so for a topic; in another, lively student questions enlarged the content; and a third group had to review the ideas again and again. This continual adjustment to circumstance corresponds to the way actors vary their tempo in order to accommodate the pulse of the audience.

Thus both teaching and acting are interactive arts. As good actors alter their timing, emphasis, and delivery to accommodate the nuances of each performance, good teachers watch faces with a practiced eye, by-passing or reiterating in response to student reaction. In both arts, the practitioners who are unable to judge the effect of what they are saying and doing are at a considerable disadvantage.

Walter Kerr, a distinguished drama critic, described the role of the audience (and, by extrapolation, students) as follows:

> It doesn't just mean that we are in the personal presence of performers. It means that they are in *our* presence, conscious of us, speaking to us, working for and with us until a circuit that is not mechanical becomes established between us, a circuit that is fluid, unpredictable, ever-changing in its impulses, crackling, intimate. *Our* presence, the way we respond, flows back to the performer and alters what he does, to some degree and sometimes astonishinglyso, every single night. We are contenders, making the play and the evening and the emotion together. We are playmates, building a structure.[2]

Finally, to note one further analogy, academic classes and theater audiences are both groups and thus subject to the contagious behavior associated with crowd psychology. As individuals, we act alone. As group members, we act in consort. When we are uncertain as to the right thing to do, we often pattern our behavior after that of others. Teachers and actors alike, therefore, must reckon not with the person but rather with the mass.

In groups, humor, sorrow, and even comprehension are infectious. When those around us show shock, we try to understand the cause; and once we understand, we are likely to follow suit. When others smile, we sense that something amusing has occurred, and we endeavor to share in the joke. And when the most perceptive students in a class radiate delight, having assimilated a complicated idea, they turn to their slower classmates and exhort, "Don't you get it? It's simple!" Encouraged in this way, others renew their efforts and soon share the smile of understanding. Learners, one could say, are the teacher's audience! They become a crowd, in the sociological sense, when they identify with one another, exhibit common values, and reflect similar attitudes.

A second set of likenesses between classroom and theater stems from parallels in the forms of communication used by actors and teachers. Both communicate through nonverbal, as well as verbal, messages. The actor draws taut to show tension; the teacher frowns to indicate dissatisfaction. In classrooms the world over, sharply clapped hands instantly command student attention; a pencil rapped on a desk reduces noise; and a finger shaken in the air serves as a sign of warning. Students, in fact, learn early on to read the nonverbal clues of their teachers. I was seated, on one occasion, in the rear of a junior high school classroom, waiting with the students for the teacher, who was a few moments late. Upon her entry, a youngster seated directly in front of me took one look and abruptly broke off a conversation with a friend. "Cool it!" he whispered. "There's going to be trouble!" Sure enough, midway through the period, the teacher reprimanded a boy for some inconsequential matter.

At the end of the period, I could barely contain myself. Uttering a brief thank you to the teacher, I chased the youngster down the hall. Catching up with him, I said:

"I'm curious. How did you know there would be trouble?"

"What?" he answered with a blank look.

"When the teacher came in, you looked at her, and told your friend there would be trouble."

"Oh!" he replied with a smile. "She wore the blue dress!"

"I don't understand," I said, puzzled.

"There's trouble whenever she wears the blue dress," he explained. "The first time she wore it, we had to stay after school. The second time she wore it, she sent Pete to the office. And the third time, we got extra homework. Whenever she wears the blue dress, there's trouble."

Teachers and actors also make extensive use of metaphor, relying heavily upon the imagination of their observers. Watching a performance of Ibsen's *Doll House*, for example, the audience must visualize the environment symbolized by the stage set. Similarly, a teacher may say: "Suppose we were all aboard a ship, and the crew became ill. What would be the best thing to do?" In both instances, the students and the audience must use imagery to become involved. Metaphor also allows teachers and actors to communicate more vividly by representing the unfamiliar with the familiar. Even colloquial phrases like "What a turkey," or "Beethoven turns me on," or "The trip was a real bummer," help convey meaning. When the shop teacher bellows, "Knock it off!" his students do not take him literally: they recognize that he wants some misbehavior to stop rather than to have an object dislodged. In the classroom, metaphor is particularly advantageous in simulations (themselves a form of drama) and in role playing.

Teaching and acting, when elevated to an art, also require an aptitude for improvisation. The teacher adds to the text and the actor to the script. Personal ingenuity, in the form of elegant embellishments, becomes a resource for intensifying impact and reducing inattentiveness. The actor may devise a gesture and the teacher may create an exercise; both serve the same purpose: to enhance effectiveness.

Theater and classroom also make deliberate use of tension. In plays, intrigue springs from conflict, suspense, and confrontation. Once baited, the audience wants to find out who wins, who loses, whether the villain receives his just desserts. In classrooms, tests, debates, contests (which table will be ready first), and the search for right answers, also evoke tension. Without a bit of constructive stress, the organism's full machinery is not put to use. To create tension, in fact, skillful teachers often exploit an element of mystery incorporate in the topic. "Tomorrow," they say, "we will at last find out which of the two candidates became president!" Or they may entice interest with some other unknown: "Who do you think will win the war?" they ask quizzically, or, "Can the color *really* change?" Curiosity is a powerful motivator. The instructor, or playwright, who fails to take advantage of its potential may encounter consciousness-lowering rather than consciousness-raising.

Another commonality exists in what in theater is known as a "play of ideas." Dramas are sometimes built around an intellectual problem or social issue. The playwright seeks to make a statement or to set forth a point of view, and the play serves as a vehicle for the author's commentary. Teachers also attempt, at various times, to make their classes aware of a societal dilemma. Even upper-elementary students can, when properly led, become interested in intellectual issues.

In such situations, the teacher serves as a dramaturgist. If, for example, she draws the students' attention to political repression in a foreign nation and then asks what might happen if the U.S. tried to help by permitting open immigration, a drama-like scenario is set. Or, when the instructor asks—after a discussion on energy and pollution problems—whether changing to electric cars would be desirable, a social problem is again given a bit of dramatic impetus.

Both the theater and the classroom are dependent on inner vitality—a sort of core energy that generates a centripetal force. Without this force, both are likely to be sterile. In a play, for example, the scenery and costuming may be spectacular, the acting solid, and the plot believable. But if internal drive is absent, the drama will lack momentum and interest. The same is true of classrooms: the lesson plan may be sensible, good instructional activities used, and the teaching respectable, yet the learning does not get anywhere. Everyone engages in the proper motions but there is no spirit or soul. If, however, something serendipitous ignites a spark, the lesson suddenly comes to life.

Actor and teacher are critical agents in their respective enterprises. The actor interprets the playwright's message, making it comprehensible; and the teacher makes learning viable. Until the instructor takes hold, the classroom is moribund. Books, paper, chalk, and maps are all inconsequential unless the teacher fashions them into a vital force. What is crucial beyond all else—in theater and classrooms—is eliciting a response to the artist's performance. School and theater are made vibrant or lifeless by the way teachers and actors function.

A central element in the work of actors and teachers is the ability to judge the audience. The collective mood must be interpreted, receptivity gauged, and timing adjusted. More, both actor and teacher must determine the right level of intensity and the best way to sustain participant involvement. Both must project themselves in a manner that heightens audience involvement. Playgoers quickly recognize an inept performer, much as students (experienced teacher-watchers) readily detect an uncertain or incompetent instructor. There are teachers, for example, who seem to teach as if no one was there. Their behavior is dry, the assignments perfunctory, and there is no effort to fine tune the procedures to situations or to student moods.

One of the difficulties that constantly bedevils teachers is that of stimulating enthusiasm. To make the students willing allies, the teacher must provide some sort of shelter against alienation and persuade them that the task is worthwhile. Such persuasion, however, is not always easy. In training actors, the gifted teacher Constantine Stanislavski used two techniques to increase realism. Through a device he called the "magic if," he asked actors to imagine themselves involved in a particular incident. "What if," for example, "I suddenly won a lottery. How would I feel?" Or, "What if I had a flat tire, during a cold, wintry night, on a lonely road? What would I do?'' By using their imaginations, and attempting to actually feel themselves in these situations, the actors' performance often became more believable.

His other technique was even more relevant to classroom teaching. Stanislavski asked his actors to recall a past event in their lives, similar to the one they were trying to enact. All human feelings, he argued, stem from previous experience. By recalling this experience, and reliving the impact, the actors were able to emulate natural behavior and the acting became more realistic. Using the same trick, effective teachers sometimes think back to their own school days, imagine themselves in a parallel situation, and recall what they would have liked to have happen. If the recollection is sufficiently powerful, memory furnishes answers, and they can then invoke tactics which are exactly right.

It is clear, therefore, that teachers are constantly on stage. They ''act'' to bring about the ends they seek. Those who act with greater skill are more likely to accomplish their intent.

Another parallel between teaching and acting lies in the structural similarities of classrooms and theaters. People on stage do things: they function with premeditated intention. Teachers in classrooms also act intentionally: they read, write, talk, solve problems, and stir about, accomplishing various tasks. Their intent is to make learning an active process. Indeed, an old aphorism holds that ''we learn by doing.'' And so we do. The surest sign of a poor classroom is a perverted relationship between the teaching and the learning. When the teacher is perpetually active—and the student forever passive—the results are but a pale facsimile of what could be. Human behavior, on the stage and in the learning hall, must be orchestrated so that maximal effect is obtained.

For all of the parallels, one very important difference separates school and stage. Although a theater audience may become intellectually and emotionally involved, they remain observers, witnessing rathering than entering into the action. In the classroom, however, the student is a coperformer rather than a vicarious onlooker. Moreover, while the actor follows the script, the teacher continually revises it to fit the learners' response. Teachers need considerable skill in interactive improvisation—the continual refining of the pedagogy to correspond with the situations that evolve. Thus teachers must function as playwrights, directors, and actors. They emulate playwrights when they organize a lesson; they behave like directors when they orchestrate the various components of the instruction; and they become actors when they execute the teaching itself.

Artist teachers perform their roles imaginatively, so as to enlarge what is organic in the learning situation. Surfeit quickly follows sufficiency, of course, and excessive histrionics are more of a liability than an asset. But to not act at all would be to yield all vestige of vitality, charisma, and persuasiveness.

The way teachers act, moreover, establishes personal style. Style, as Kenneth Eble notes in his beautiful book *A Perfect Education*, is a special way of being.[3] It is reflected in what teachers choose to do, and in the way they do it. Style not only gives a teacher individuality; it is the quality that most attracts or repels students. Style is apparent, not just in dress and habit, but in values and character as well. It is style, above all else, that makes for distinctive performance.

Style, whether embodied in an eccentricity, a special mannerism, or a particular passion, is proclaimed in the way teachers act. Acting is the means by which they convey their convictions and beliefs, and their way of doing things. Even if it were possible to teach without acting, the performance would be devoid of color, energy, and intrigue.

In the crafts of acting and teaching, the artist conveys an image of self. There are those, I suppose, who will find inconsistency in my use of ''art'' and ''craft.'' I must confess that I have never quite understood the effort to separate the two. For artistry exists in carpentry and sewing fully as much as in teaching and painting. Artistry, in short, is mastery carried to the ultimate. It is executing any human endeavor with such extraordinary grace, precision, and efficiency that the performance itself takes on aesthetic beauty. Teachers and actors project—through their method of functioning—a personal portrait. By the use—or nonuse—of particular words and gestures, idioms, body movements, pursuits, and aims, they define themselves for their observers. Although actors create characters, and teachers personify characters, they make use of similar communication tools.

And, at the risk of laboring the obvious, teachers and actors both act. All the world may not be a stage, but acting is part and parcel of everyday life. All of us, for example, play social roles.

We expect the store clerk to be attentive and courteous. As mothers and fathers, we enact parenthood. Most of us, in fact, are always—consciously or unconsciously—playing a role. The games in Eric Berne's famous *Games People Play* are really a form of acting.[4]

Acting is not pretense. It is used not to deceive, but rather to vivify. Teachers act in order to gain attention, to clarify, and to stimulate. They do not attempt to portray something they are not, but instead to convince by dramatizing. Moreover, though their repute has ebbed and flowed in recent times, teachers as models are imitated, followed, and adored by children. As such, they must act in ways that meet the social expectations of the community and the personal needs of their students. The first grader who needs a reassuring hug and the distraught mother who needs to be heartened about a temporary bedwetting problem both feel entitled to the services teachers render. I have long wondered, in this regard, why we are so prone to take fine teachers casually. Their force goes far beyond reading, arithmetic, and spelling. Few of us have been untouched by the ministrations—or lack of them—of a teacher who at one point or another was important to us. Now and then, in a cursory moment of candor, we may hear someone acknowledge that it was Sister Loretta, or perhaps old Miss Douglas, "who taught me the value of putting your best foot forward." The role expectations of supporter, advocate, friend, and tutor are deeply embedded in our concept of "teacher."

Teaching is a performing art for the simple—but compelling—reason that the desire to learn is strongly affected by the teacher's behavior. Therefore, to achieve their purpose, gifted instructors make use not only of sound pedagogical principles, but also of ideas that come from the stuff of their own psychic attics. They take advantage of spontaneity, nonverbal communication, and role playing to ensure that learning goes beyond inert understanding. Comprehension, in a sense, is a compromise between the child's capacities and the teacher's ability to harness them constructively. It is instinct that prompts inspired teaching. Although there is reason for concern when entertainment substitutes for education, an appealing style and imaginative performance can greatly increase the teacher's effectiveness. The right kind of theatrics heightens interest, underscores matters of significance, and gives learning an element of excitement. The use of dramatic emphasis, in addition, allows teachers to express their own creativeness and to vivify their personal approach to instruction.

To give some sort of structure to the teachers' pedagogical inventions in our experiment, four concepts were borrowed from the world of theater. There are striking similarities between the unfolding of a dramatic plot and the unraveling of an intellectual mystery. The teachers were asked occasionally during their teaching to (1) develop instructional "scenarios" or dramatic episodes that could be used to arouse student interest, (2) function as an actor while teaching, (3) organize their procedures in ways that would make the classroom more exciting for the student, and (4) construct games or other "intrigues" that would help sustain learner attention during drill and practice periods. The four concepts can be illustrated schematically:

Four Themes of Artistry in Teaching

1. *Dramatic Episodes*	2. *Teaching as Acting*
Teacher *improvising* which	Conscious role *portraying* based on
attracts learner attention increases student motivation dramatizes lesson objectives illustrates intellectual concepts	personal teaching style appealing classroom personality teaching procedures that enhance: —alertness —interest —enthusiasm —persistence

3. *Classroom Atmosphere*	4. *Classroom Staging*
Creating and stimulating learning *environment* wherein students sense teacher	*Creating* learning activities that
dedication perseverance compassion excellence	reduce boredom provoke curiosity increase motivation improve classroom order reinforce cognitive understanding

Each of the four themes focused on teaching behavior that heightens student incentive. The dramatic episodes were used to induce greater responsiveness by playing up the usefulness, or intrigue, of a learning objective. Similarly, the attempts by teachers to act in ways which increased student interest in what was going on served—directly and indirectly—as a motivational prod. The classroom atmosphere factors, related primarily to the manner in which learning activities were organized, allowed teachers to choose arrangements that symbolized a receptive climate, concern for student welfare, and a caring attitude. Lastly, the staging devices were designed to flag sagging attention and to revitalize enthusiasm.

During the early stages of the experiments, in a further integration of theatrical and teaching technique, a number of teachers were paired with specialists in the dramatic arts. The use of theater specialists was somewhat unpremeditated. My original thought was that occasional touches of drama would enliven classroom life. Since teachers do not study dramatics during their training, opportunities for a bit of flourish here and there often are overlooked. Formal instruction in theater was inappropriate, but a loose collaboration with someone experienced in the theater might open teachers' eyes to the possibilities of dramatic pedagogy.

The nature of the theater is such that virtually everyone connected with it eventually develops a certain flair. Actor, director, and producer alike acquire, as a consequence of long exposure, a sensitivity to what will, or will not, hold attention. In view of this, I decided to invite individuals familiar with the theater to work with teachers in plotting more enlivened approaches to teaching. To find such people, I turned to college and university drama departments, television studios, little theater groups, and professional acting schools. A good many people were willing to sit down with a teacher for an hour or so to help work on an interesting classroom presentation. Those who volunteered were perhaps motivated by the challenge, or possibly by memories of their own boredom in school.

In reality, I needed to do little more than supply the teachers with names of local specialists and ask them to arrange meetings. In the partnerships which followed, some met for lunch or dinner; a few consultants actually visited the teachers at school;

and—in one of the happy peculiarities of fate—it turned out, in the Chicago area, that a teacher and a television studio assistant director lived three houses apart. There was, in addition, a good deal of interaction by telephone.

When they met, the teachers would describe their classes, explain the topic involved, and pinpoint a specific teaching objective. The specialist then tried, either immediately or after a few days of reflection, to suggest a dramatic vehicle. In the give-and-take which ensued, a tentative solution usually was reached.

The results of the collaboration were variable: a few ended relatively quickly because the specialist lost interest; some failed to jell at all because the consultant was unable to come up with anything constructive; and some survived and even deepened over time. The specialists' suggestions were equally disparate: one teacher taught a series of weekly value sessions through classroom discussions on the TV program "All in the Family"; another conducted a similar analysis of "Mash" episodes. One imaginative consultant persuaded a teacher to assign her students the production of radio commercials communicating important principles in science. A good number of recommendations resulted in various kinds of game shows, also patterned after those on television, which were used to test knowledge of the material studied. In two different cities, neophyte comedians visited classrooms presumably seeking captive audiences with which to practice. The hope was that, through humor, important ideas could be driven home more firmly. Although the students enjoyed both performances, only one of the teachers felt the comedy actually reinforced substantive understanding.

Besides the difficulty of arranging meeting times between the teachers and theater specialists, there were other problems with this portion of the experiment. The dramatic scenarios conjured up by the specialists were often too elaborate and time consuming. As a result, many teachers were unwilling to interrupt their instructional schedule. Conversely, an occasional teacher became so carried away with the staging devices that learning suffered. In retrospect, I concluded that the use of theater consultants probably was impractical. Nonetheless, I was also convinced that it would be beneficial to incorporate exercises in dramatic presentation in the training of teachers. The collaboration efforts also reinforced my belief that practitioners' minds can be opened to new motivational possibilities.

There were somewhat similar outcomes in the "Teaching as Acting" phase. The effect of physical manner and body language in commanding attention is well documented. Many teachers not only fail to exploit their potential but, worse, adopt a classroom presence that is singularly uninspiring. Few of us, in fact, have been spared the ordeal of a listless instructor. It therefore seemed reasonable that a little professional coaching in presence and in the physical and psychological techniques of capturing children's interest through movement would be useful to teachers.

Subsequent discussions with drama experts suggested that training which enabled teachers to register emotion—surprise, disbelief, disappointment, joy—would be of greatest utility in this regard. I arranged in three locales, during the early phases, to offer a workshop in instructional behavior for teachers. Organized through the university extension department and led by a professor who routinely taught classes in acting, the workshops met the usual requirements for professional inservice training. Nine people enrolled in the smallest, and twenty-one in the largest, of the three workshops. Generally, the content paralleled that in an introductory acting course, modified somewhat to fit the roles of teachers. Although the three instructors varied somewhat in their comparative emphasis on voice projection, body control, and other fundamentals, essentially the same matter was covered.

The results, much as in the use of the theater specialists, were neither a clear success nor failure. Teachers differed in their opinions of the workshops' value: some had more natural aptitude than others; a number emerged from the training with the belief that their effectiveness had increased considerably; and a percentage reached the conclusion that acting had no place in teaching. The two things which seemed most clear were, first, that elementary teachers found the training more valuable than secondary teachers, and, second, that almost all of the teachers thought the workshops interesting.

To verify these findings, as well as to test the possibilities a second time, I arranged for one of the twenty schools in Phase Two to also take an acting workshop. It produced the same mixed results; differing estimates of worth, divided reactions, and inconclusive data. It would be irrational, hence, to advocate—from the evidence—thespian training for teachers. But, at the same time, it cannot be denied that, while artist teachers are not actors per se, a good many gifted pedagogues owe part of their excellence to an aptitude for drama which holds student attention.

Taken as a whole, the experiment did not yield a definitive theory of artistry in teaching. A great deal was learned, however, about the questions which prompted the study. Finesse, for example, *can* be extended through practice and, certainly, learners react with greater enthusiasm to instruction which stirs their emotions. Of greatest importance, possibly, the venture cast more light on those subtle and elusive qualities which make for exceptional performance in teaching.

Many of the teachers derived considerable satisfaction from their role as experimentalists. Aware that the project sought to discover whether their own insights could be merged with scientific research in improving the practice of teaching, they took their involvement seriously. There were occasional exceptions, as might be expected, but by and large those who participated made genuine efforts to think analytically about teaching problems and to find imaginative solutions.

What follows, in the next four chapters, is a description of the four themes—dramatic episodes, teaching as acting, classroom mood, and lesson staging—which were used to stimulate artistry during the experiments. Artistic teaching, it should be clear, requires far more than theatrical devices. Firm control, good organization, efficient procedures, and dedication, for example, are all indispensable. The themes were intended to demonstrate the importance of excitement in learning, and to show how ''it'' fits into the overall technical repertory of master teachers.

9

DRAMATIC EPISODES

Encapsulating a lesson or a concept in a dramatic situation may be extremely useful. Properly managed, it can provoke excitement, increase learner attention, sustain motivation, and intensify the relevance of a lesson. Moreover, an element of drama can be introduced by involving students, in real or simulated social problems, by demonstrating scientific phenomena, by playing intellectual games, and by virtually any other constructive maneuver that helps to offset tedium or engender suspense.

Now and then, the teachers used their "dramatic episodes" to convey the cognitive ideas inherent in a lesson. More often, however, they served as a "hook" to either bait or increase student interest. At times, the episode was employed at the beginning of a unit to stimulate student curiosity, and at other times it was used during the reinforcement stage, to dramatize relevance and reduce student lethargy. Provocatively presented, even a concept as cheerless as verb tense can be made captivating.

Theatrical situations can be found in stories, riddles, psychodramas, charades, and puzzles—in any contrivance that (a) commands student attention and (b) illustrates a learning principle. The episodes were not intended as a substitute for other teaching procedures. They were designed, rather to "spark up" conventional pedagogy, to facilitate pacing, and, through enticement, to coax student involvement. The teachers were reminded, again and again, that although the theatrics were motivationally useful, they could not replace problem solving, analysis, lecture, discussion, memorization, and the other indispensable tools of good teaching.

These motivational spurs—incentives to learn—stem from a variety of sources. Some are spawned by teacher threat or student fear of failure. Others, set loose by conscious or unconscious factors, spring from a situation which incites interest. The use of drama in teaching is based upon this latter kind of incentive. Teaching "scenarios" help engage the mind, energize greater cognitive activity, and—because they are captivating—lure the learner's attention. Any classroom occurrence or event that achieves these effects constitutes a dramatic episode.

It was a conventional seventh-grade social studies unit on community government. While the discussion of city administration progressed, a red-headed lad seated near the outside wall gazed absently out the window.

"Larry!"

The boy's gaze turned quickly to the teacher.

"You don't seem very interested in city councils," Mr. Gallardo said pleasantly.

A sheepish look crossed the student's face.

"I don't blame him," a girl aross the room muttered. "All this stuff is dumb!"

"Why?" Mr. Gallardo asked.

A silence fell.

"How many of you really think what we've been talking about is dumb?" the teacher asked again insistently.

The girl who had complained finally thrust her hand into the air, glancing challengingly at her classmates. Somewhat hesitantly, a few more hands followed. Soon, roughly half the class had raised hands.

The teacher looked thoughtful. "I'll tell you what: let's try something different. I want each row to reassemble for group discussion."

Obligingly, the students shifted their chairs and soon were arranged in five circular discussion groups.

"Now," the teacher said, "Let's assume each group is a city council. I'll give you a typical problem; you discuss it; agree on a recommendation; then we'll compare the results. O.K.?"

The class nodded.

"Very well," Mr. Gallardo said. "Here's the problem: as you may have read in last week's paper, our county land fill is almost full. We've got to start another one. Where's the best place to put it? Over by the football stadium, near the interstate, next to the old homes on Elm Street, where? Remember now, wherever it's put, some people are going to be very unhappy. There will be a lot of truck noise, trees and other vegetation will have to be removed, there could be some powerful odors, and the value of the houses near the new land fill might go down."

He smiled encouragingly at the class: "O.K." he said, "decide where to put it."

Slowly, at first, and then more animatedly, the discussions began. Soon there was a hum of debate. Twenty minutes later, Mr. Gallardo halted the discussions and asked a representative from each group to summarize the conclusions. There was considerable disagreement.

As the period came to an end, the teacher said: "Tomorrow we'll compare and analyze each group's suggestions."

The students left the room still talking about a good place for a land fill.

Although the teacher's use of simulation was not spectacular in its originality—problem-solving approaches to instruction have been widely used for years—the artistry was apparent in his shrewd recognition that the lesson had become tiresome, in his instinctive realization that one student's disengagement would soon spread to others, and in his ability to deviate from the planned instructional sequence with an impromptu adjustment. Four distinct aspects of master craftsmanship are reflected in the teacher's ploy: a knowledge of simulation technique; a sensitivity to classroom pulse; a willingness to extemporize; and a skillful transition between the planned and unplanned aspects of the lesson.

Used at whatever points the teachers thought advisable, the episodes sometimes were as brief as three minutes and sometimes as long as several weeks. A teacher might, for example, preempt student attention with brief task (think of twenty ways to use burnt-out light bulbs) or sustain interest throughout a unit of study (write a series of letters to American embassy officials in foreign countries, inquiring how other nations react to United States foreign policy). The measure of a device's merit was the extent to which it heightened attentiveness. And the real test of heightened attentiveness was improved learning—improved in the sense that more information was assimilated, a deeper conceptual understanding was achieved, and skills were developed with greater efficiency.[1] Thus, although the episodes clearly were designed to be entertaining, entertainment was not their primary purpose.

In emphasizing theatrical maneuvers, the objective was to awaken dormant talent and unfetter teachers' capacities for improvisation. They were familiarized with a number of models and given sample collections of tactics that could be used in different contexts. This was done to demonstrate, in a very direct way, the benefits of enlivening instruction through dramatic elements. Short profiles, similar to those in this volume, were made available. Basically, the profiles described a typical teaching situation, the teacher's stylistic inclinations, and an artistic device—either successful or unsuccessful—that had been tried.

The teachers working in groups also shared their own inventions. Some would have been content to acquire, at second hand, an assemblage of gimmicks for their bag of professional tricks. Since, however, the goal was to resurrect their creative talents—which had been largely dormant—reliance upon prefabricated techniques was discouraged and there was a press for the continuous development of new ones.

Aside from pointing out that an infinite number of methods could be used by the teacher to rouse and sustain student attention—learners, for example, can be motivated by a bit of friendly competition, by something that interjects an element of fun, by suddenly sensing the power of an idea—no particular instructions were given. The teachers were told that a provocative learning stimulus could be harnessed to any teaching aim. Pains were taken, however, to convince the participants that test scores ought not be the sole criteria of instructional effectiveness. If, as a case in point, children learn through an instructional system in reading to decode and comprehend language symbols, but fail to grasp, as well, the joy of reading for pleasure, the instruction is less than perfect, however high the students' performance on standardized achievement assessments.

I also stressed that inspired teaching makes use of the unexpected. Children have a natural sense of curiosity and wonder, and learning which brings surprise, or overturns existing notions, is therefore especially exciting. As the teachers and their theater consultants sought to improvise teaching vehicles, they were urged to look for ideas which would dispel a misconception, expose an unsuspected fact, or provide a new insight. For example a lesson that allows children to realize that one can become tanned on a cloudy day—and to understand why—carries an element of excitement and a delight in further intellectual discovery.

Theorists who study teaching have long conjectured whether a certain amount of fun is an instructional asset. Since students are able to learn in a variety of ways, and since they also tend to find some learning experiences more interesting than others, the question is whether the added dimensions of pleasure and attraction offer psychological advantage. A Harvard law professor, for example, appeared in a Boston television program called "Miller's Court." The program, designed to teach basic legal principles to viewers, is an outgrowth of his Harvard lectures. A highly respected scholar, Professor Miller is not above entertaining his students with dramatic skits, organizing controversial debates, and even appearing in costume for his classroom lectures.[2]

Not surprisingly, his courses are exceedingly popular. While the students are not entirely convinced that they learn more than they would through prosaic teaching, they readily acknowledge that the learning process is infinitely more appealing. One cannot help but wonder, nonetheless, whether perhaps greater learning does occur. Pedagogically, Professor Miller's techniques are easily analyzed: he makes abundant use of debate (Should aliens have the same constitutional rights as citizens?), provokes his students through skillful questions, and—by avoiding closure on issues—leaves them with something to think about. It is this post-instructional thinking that may make more difference than the students perceive. For once our interest has been piqued, and we become fascinated with a problem, there is a strong lure to continued reflective thinking. It is this satisfaction in ongoing engagement which may, over time, lead to greater insight and wisdom.

Researchers have recently investigated lost instructional time. There is considerable dissipation, they suggest, between the time allocated for learning a subject, the amount of time actually used for teaching in this allocated period, and the time the students "attend" or pay attention to what is going on during the teaching. If, as an example, forty minutes are assigned to a science lesson, but the teacher uses ten of the forty minutes for noninstructional purposes (distributing materials, maintaining order, answering questions about homework) and, in addition, the learners also are inattentive during ten of the forty minutes, there is a cumulative loss of twenty instructional minutes.

Dramatic episodes—and to an extent all four of the theater-connected devices—help reduce such loss. By invoking greater student interest, they increase the amount of time students are involved. Television commercials, as an illustration, habitually use some form of action, other than the product itself, to attract attention. A picture of a package of dog food does not hold the viewer's interest beyond a second or two, but two dogs racing toward the food may lure the audience into watching for the outcome. In short, peripheral stimuli, if not excessive, greatly increase concentration.[3] Gifted teachers consequently use artful bait of one sort or another to prolong learner absorption. A clever instructor may resurrect waning interest in a science lesson by casually observing: "I've heard it said that eightly percent of all the scientists who have existed are now alive. Could this be possible?" The surprise of the statement provokes a lively debate, resulting in renewed student animation, which after a few minutes is refocused on the objectives of the lesson.

The human capacity for focus is limited, even more in children than adults. Moreover, when a study topic is not inherently enthralling, students are especially apt to turn their thoughts elsewhere. Anything, therefore, which prods interest or arouses curiosity helps to lengthen the amount of time they remain attentive. Thus the teacher with a wary eye for boredom who—in the midst of a discussion that has lost its fire—says: "If the class gets the next three questions right, I'll start the art period early," instantly stimulates interest in both the challenge itself and the desire to learn the resolution.

The chief distinction between dramatic episodes and the classroom staging maneuvers described in Chapter 12 lies in the teacher's intent. For reasons of clarity, the participants in the experiments were asked to devise bits of drama which could pique the students' mental aquisitiveness at the beginning of a unit and staging activities which would reactivate alertness at some midpoint in the unit when signs of boredom appeared. For all practical purposes, however, most of the devices invented were inter-changeable: they could be used whenever the teacher wished. The time, in sum, was of less consequence than the lure. An illustration which I have often used in lectures is perhaps appropriate here:

"Before we begin the next science chapter," the teacher said, "I'd like to tell you a story. Then," she added with a slight smile, "I'll ask you a question."

The sixth graders looked at their teacher expectantly.

"A man was out driving in his car," the teacher began, "when he noticed something quite unusual. A truck stopped in the middle of a block, and the truck driver got out with a baseball bat in his hands. He walked back to the center of the truck and suddenly hit the side several times with the bat. Then he got back in and drove on."

Several children who had been somewhat indifferent when the teacher started now looked at her raptly.

"As the man in the car followed the truck," she continued, "he saw the truck again stop, after about three blocks, and again the driver got out, beat his truck a few times with the bat, returned to his seat, and drove off."

Every eye in the room was now riveted on the teacher.

"Once more," the teacher went on, "the man in the car followed the truck and, sure enough, in another three blocks it stopped, the driver got out and banged away with his bat."

The teacher paused and glanced around the room. Satisfied that she had the class's attention, she continued. "The man in the car," she said, "was fascinated. He followed the truck for almost two miles, trying to figure out what the truck driver was doing. Finally, he gave up."

The teacher again paused, scanning the intent faces in front of her.

"The next time the truck stopped" she went on, "the man jumped out of his car, ran over to the truck driver, and said: 'Sir, forgive me for bothering you. But I've been following you for almost two miles. Why on earth do you drive exactly three blocks, get out with a baseball bat, and hit your truck a few times?' The truck driver said, 'It's really very simple. I've got a two-ton truck and inside I've got three tons of canaries. So, I've got to keep one ton of them in the air at all times.'

A few of the students looked puzzled, some seemed skeptical, and several laughed. As the teacher waited, the laughter gradually spread until the entire class was smiling.

"Now," she said, "let me give you a question."

Looking pointedly at the class, she asked, "Was the truck driver stupid?"

There was a sudden silence as the children pondered the query.
"Yes," a sandy-haired boy said suddenly. "He still had three tons in
his truck."
The teacher remained silent, watching her students. Then a bright-
eyed girl in the corner of the room raised her hand shyly.
"Beth."
"He really wasn't stupid," the girl said. "Because if one ton was fly-
ing around inside the truck, they wouldn't add any weight."
With this, the teacher smiled and walked to the board. She then began
a lesson on the principle of air support.

We sometimes forget that entertainment can teach, and teaching can entertain. Students become interested in whatever seems personally relevant or exciting. The best of teachers, consequently, excel at presenting their subject matter in ways that catch their students' fancy. They may require their classes to memorize, to undergo systematic testing, to drill and practice, but they nonetheless take the trouble to incite, inspire, and captivate. They use amusement and entertainment not as substitutes but as catalysts. The sweetening of an otherwise bitter pill strikes them as patently logical. They know that an idea made more appealing, or easier to grasp, need not lose its potency. Hence they make extensive use of ploys which tempt the learner's mind.[4]

As teachers go, Larry Dobbs is virtually devoid of color. Earnest and straightforward, he wears neat, nondescript clothing; speaks with a monotonous, slightly nasal twang; and follows each of his lesson plans religiously, without the slightest deviation. Although pleasant and agreeable, he seems totally immersed in routine. Watching him work, one has the feeling that he has risen at the same hour, eaten the same breakfast, and driven the same route every day of his life.

He volunteered for the artistry program because—as he himself put it—"no one needs it more than I do." Mr. Dobbs was unable, during the first seven weeks, to create a single artistic gambit. Ideas occurred to him but he was unable to organize them. For the first month or so, his colleagues were encouraging but, as the days passed without any signs of progress, they quietly decided that Larry just wasn't the artistic type. When he was in the teachers' lounge, they tactfully refrained from talking about the experiment.

Fate, however, works in strange ways. One afternoon Larry

was late for his car pool. The others, assuming that he had other plans, were just driving away when Larry ran into the parking lot. The car had gone perhaps 150 feet when Larry whistled. It was, by all reports, a truly incredible whistle: traffic in the vicinity stopped momentarily, children on the playground interrupted their games, and several people stared at Larry with astonishment. His target—the car-pool vehicle—also halted abruptly. As Larry entered, a counselor in the back seat said "Wow! You ought to try that whistle in class. Your kinds would really get turned on!"

This idle suggestion apparently took hold, for a week or so later, Larry, pleased with a student's astute answer to a question, cut loose with another blast. His students, needless to say, were delighted. From that point on, especially good answers were rewarded with one of Larry's ear-splitting emissions. Soon, his students started a contest to see who could win the greatest number of whistles. At the time the incident was related to me, a slim redheaded girl was leading the class with thirteen.

It would seem that virtually anything which helps to alleviate monotony constitutes a step toward artistry.

10

TEACHER AS ACTOR

Many of our finest teachers, managing truly superb classrooms, are not particularly good actors or actresses. They are neither flashy nor spectacular; they do not seem to create special effects; and their procedures are relatively straightforward. Yet, when observed in their classrooms, they display a certain flair. Potential disruptions, for example, are defused before they develop; shifts from one learning activity to another occur effortlessly; sagging student attention is revived with a casual question or movement, and learner fatigue is notably absent. Consequently, there is good reason to believe that making teachers more aware of "presence" and personal impact is not without value.

Accumulated research evidence reveals that highly successful instructors exhibit a number of relatively consistent characteristics: enthusiasm, alertness, persistence, clarity.[1] We hoped, therefore, that teachers could find ways to emphasize these qualities and to use teaching as a means of self-expression. The quest was not to train teachers to play prescribed roles but to help them develop personalized styles. While we pointed out that teachers periodically could simulate emotion (anger, empathy, contentment, despair, delight) through judicious use of theatrics, in order to "turn on" their students, we also suggested that affectations of this sort were only a means to an end—contrivances to be used sparingly—when the time was right. In essence, the stress upon "teacher as actor" was aimed at making the teacher a more intriguing classroom personality.

Whether classroom personality is distinct from general personality is debatable. Certainly the two are related: a vivacious, bubbly person is not likely to have a listless classroom manner. Whatever a teacher's native personality, nonetheless, mannerisms can be acquired which make the classroom considerably more stimulating. We know, for example, that teaching involves multiple actions, all directed toward the accomplishment of the learning objective. To the extent that some of these actions are evocative—capable of stimulating students' interest and attention—advantageous side effects occur. While other theorists have speculated about "teaching as a performing art," their emphasis has been somewhat different from mine. I was not interested in dramatics per se, or in converting teachers into actors, but rather in a practical coalescence between teaching techniques, learning processes, and the principles of drama.

There is, of course, an important difference between role portrayal in the theater and in classrooms. Actors follow a prepared script and follow the director's wishes. Teachers are not bound by assigned lines, but adapt their scenarios to the situation, organizing, monitoring, and redirecting activities as necessary. And they play a role by acting in ways intended to achieve a particular effect.

> *Having finished an explanation of simple subtraction, accompanied by chalkboard illustrations, the teacher asked the class to try a few problems in the text.*
> *The room was unusually warm, the children seemed dispirited, and the teacher sensed that the lesson was not "taking." Her suspicions were confirmed, twenty minutes later, when she announced the correct answers to the trial problems: With one or two exceptions, a majority of the students had missed most of the items.*
> *A look of despair crossed the teacher's face. Elbows on the desk, her face cupped in her hands, she stared silently, with downcast eyes, at the top of her desk.*
> *"What's the matter?" one of the children asked anxiously.*
> *The teacher remained silent.*
> *"What's wrong?" another child asked with rising concern.*
> *Again the teacher was silent.*

"Are you mad at us?" a girl inquired apprehensively.

The teacher looked up. "No," she said, "I'm just not very good today."

"What do you mean?" a sandy-haired boy asked.

"I've explained subtraction the best way I know how," the teacher observed sadly, "and you just don't get it. Maybe I shouldn't be a teacher."

A silence descended over the room. The children stared at the teacher with dismay.

"You could try one more time," a small girl said hopefully.

"What's the use?" the teacher replied dully.

"Explain it again," several students clamored.

With a shrug of resignation, the teacher returned to the chalkboard and reviewed the subtraction process. She noted, with private satisfaction, that there was intense concentration among the students. When she finished the teacher asked, "Do you want to try some more test problems?"

"Yes," a chorus of voices shouted.

This time, when the correct answers were read, the results were substantially better.

"Now you're not sorry you're a teacher, are you?" a chubby boy asked, with a huge grin.

People who are obliged to interact routinely and repeatedly often fall into the habit of informal game-playing as temporary diversion. This is frequently the case in classrooms where a mutual feeling of fondness and respect exists between students and teacher. As part of such game-playing, a mild amount of pretense sometimes is used to enliven events. A teacher may, for example, feign horror when her students fail to tidy the room at the end of the day. Delighted by their teacher's exaggerated display of consternation, children may deliberately leave a small mess, wait for the teacher's dramatic outburst, then happily complete the clean-up activities. The game will not work, obviously, if either teacher or class are unwilling to participate.

In the foregoing illustration, the teacher pretending despair over her own incompetence was making use of a similar ploy. Whether all the students were taken in by her behavior is not of significance; those who were not undoubtedly went along with the game anyway. What is important is that the teacher (a) coaxed maximum student attention, (b) used a clever means of reviewing and reinforcing the learning objectives, (c) increased student incentive, and (d) achieved active student involvement in a game-like encounter—all in all, a rather impressive piece of pedagogical maneuvering.

The calculated use of affected behavior—or what might be called "feigned reaction"—is neither deceptive nor dishonest in spirit when the purpose is altruistic. It is, in fact, an important dimension of human interchange. Husbands and wives at times listen to one another with "obvious" interest when their minds are actually elsewhere. A telephone operator, outraged by an abusive customer, continues to speak with courteous deference. A distracted mother exhibits attentiveness because her child, bubbling with enthusiasm over some exciting event, needs desperately to share the joy with an interested parent. We often act in expected ways when we wish to satisfy the needs of others or to encourage a particular response. An animated first-grade teacher, for much the same reasons, may reflect dismay, impatience, sorrow, or pleasure in order to achieve a desired effect. Unfortunately, out of misplaced propriety, many teachers not only avoid showing emotion, they also hide or camouflage their natural feelings. In seeking to appear dignified, they instead strike their students as spiritless.

Writers use such phrases as "a colorless individual" or "a drab personality" to describe a person who is extremely uninteresting. Although blandness is by no means fatal in teaching, it can be a substantial liability. Television has accustomed children to seductive communication techniques. Students, moreover, spend long hours in schools and are invariably affected by a teacher's demeanor. Zest and vitality, for example, are usually contagious: an interesting, cheerful teacher is likely to have reasonably animated students. "Teaching as acting," consequently, has to do, among other things, with encouraging teachers to allow a bit more of their personalities to show.

Many skillful teachers exploit their own fallibility. Children are delighted when a normally accurate teacher makes a mistake. Aware of this, enterprising practitioners occasionally engage in a bit of "planned error." One would think that the proverbial absent-minded professor—because of seeming inattentiveness—automatically discourages student achievement. Preoccupation does not equal dullness, however, and more than one inspiring college instructor has been known to use minor forgetfulness effectively.

Robert M. W. Travers has suggested that effective teaching stems from "molar characteristics" such as clarity, variability, enthusiasm, and task orientation.[2] These, obviously, are performance skills. An exceedingly knowledgeable person who—although thoroughly grounded in, say, history—did not have these skills would make a poor teacher. Moreover, since such skills are acquired through practice, they can be developed to a modest, substantial, or extraordinary degree.

Many teachers have a grasp of the ideas they wish to convey, and a reasonably clear sense of role and purpose. Their pacing is unduly slow, they rely chiefly on timeworn classroom activities devoid of vitality, and they have not sharpened their classroom sensitivity. Each of these difficulties can only be overcome through a desire for excellence, deliberate effort, and systematic practice. They are learned, not through vicarious experience, but rather in the vicissitudes of reality. They can be suggested in lecture and print, but they must be mastered in the actual doing. Every teacher, therefore, must perfect a sense of timing, a feel for dramatic possibility, and an ability to exude enthusiasm in his or her own classroom by painstaking tinkering—trying this and that until the right formula evolves.[3]

In this context, essentially, the experiments on teaching as acting were established. Two particular objectives were intended: one having to do with teaching personality (presence, charisma, and behavior which captures learner interest) and one having to do with the technical skills of performance (effectiveness in giving instructions, precision in goal setting, adroitness in questioning, clarity in explaining). Said another way, teaching involves many routine procedures. Artist teachers, however, are marked by a dual distinction: they perform these routine things with uncommon grace and expertness; and they periodically escape the routine by substituting something more novel and ingenious. The hope, then, was that the experimental activities might perpetuate these attributes.

Questions of teacher acting aside, there is little doubt as to the need for the progressive mastery of instructional strategies which are rarely treated during training. The best of teachers are likely to gain these competencies on their own, without much guidance. But such development could be greatly facilitated. The experiments suggested, in fact, that frequent access to a coach,

mentor, or tutor would be particularly helpful. Just as a scale cannot weigh itself, it is exceedingly difficult for any performer—whether teacher, athlete, dancer, or lecturer—to analyze
technical strengths and weaknesses without some insight regarding the effect of the performance. Furthermore, it is one thing to
recognize that something is wrong, and quite another to know
precisely what. Most teachers, for example, can sense that a class
is getting out of hand, but many are unable to determine why. In
such instances, an adept observer, capable of canny diagnosis,
can be an aid. Of greatest import, however, the experiments
demonstrated that the ability to make rapid appraisals and decisions, to take extemporaneous advantage of a situation, and to
sense student mood may be a good deal more important in
teaching than we think.

Paul Larson teaches high school history in central Pennsylvania. In his early sixties, he is a living legend among students.
Austere in manner and punctilious in conduct, he is renowned
for his extraordinary knowledge of history, unusual mannerisms, and teaching ability.

Habitually clad in the double-breasted suits common two de-
cades ago, he shuns most pedagogical conveniences: his teaching
materials consist primarily of a roll book, the required text, and
his own considerable intelligence. In Mr. Larson's classes, tardy
students are not permitted to enter; examination scores are
posted on an announcement board at midterm and end of term,
students are addressed as Mr. Jones or Miss Smith; and the
length of a student's written assignment often is exceeded by his
personal commentary and criticism, set forth in small, precise
strokes.

Husky of build, bald, with a penchant for twirling his horn-
rimmed glasses, he presents an imposing appearance. Exact and
meticulous in action, well organized, and seemingly always in
total control, he is a great favorite of the students. While they joke
about his idiosyncrasies, they remain in awe of his wisdom, fair-
ness, and dedication to teaching. He is celebrated—among other
things—for sustaining an interesting discussion throughout the
entirety of a fire drill, when his students were supposed to vacate
the building; delivering an impromptu lecture—in the midst of an
interclass softball game—on Caesar's beliefs regarding the importance of confidence; and enrapturing a crowd seated in a federal

office for fully twenty minutes with a discourse on the virtues of limited government while they waited to see the IRS auditor regarding their income tax returns. Although he has never bothered to acquire a doctorate, Mr. Larson apparently has enough command of history to qualify for several.

Of all the teacher participants in the experiment, Paul Larson was perhaps the most cynical. During my initial presentation to his faculty, he snickered audibly when I spoke of artistic intangibles. Somewhat taken back, I asked him, point-blank, about his objections. "Good teaching," he said in a tone meant to end all further discussion, "is simply a matter of knowing your subject and student mentality." Nevertheless, I was surprised to find, when the participant sign-up sheet was returned, that he had chosen to participate.

In my subsequent visits to the school, I encountered repeated references to Paul Larson's artistry. Other teachers, in fact, urged me to visit his room. Still dubious, I chatted with him in the faculty lounge and asked him what he had contrived for the experiment. "I do something similar to Allen's TV program" he told me, "except that I play all the parts." His reference was to Steve Allen's award-winning television series "Meeting of the Minds." Securing his permission to observe, I was rewarded with a teaching performance unlike any I have ever seen, before or after.

The Allen show is based upon an imaginary debate among famous intellectuals. In a typical program, for example, Benjamin Disraeli, Leonardo da Vinci, Mary Stuart, and Alexis de Tocqueville might discuss the legitimacy of abortion. Larson—without any obvious difficulty—played each character in a similar debate. His acting was not polished, but it was convincing. In a breathtaking tour de force, he alternately described each character's comments during the imaginary discussion, or—slipping momentarily into role—spoke the lines as an actor might.

To perform this feat, it was necessary that he have an enormous grasp of the topic being argued, know a good deal about the mind bent of the individuals he portrayed, and be imaginative enough to invent dialogue. The presentation must have required hours of preparation. Experts, perhaps, might have quibbled with one statement or another, but Larson's students and I sat in hushed fascination.

The Paul Larsons of teaching, admittedly, are rare. But for those of us with more modest talents, they demonstrate that a well-informed mind is a considerable advantage, and that an understanding of ''student mentality'' is indispensable.

11

CLASSROOM ATMOSPHERE

The third of our experimental themes dealt with classroom atmosphere, the "feel" or mood of a learning environment as distinct from the charisma generated by a teacher's style. Style influences the way the classroom is organized and the strategies used in instruction. Atmosphere had to do with the psychological counterpoint and emotional ecology of the learning scene. Individuals sometimes differ in their reactions, of course, but in a good many instances, there is a universal feeling that a given classroom is either pleasant or unpleasant.

The characteristics of receptive classroom atmosphere are amorphous. They are undergirded, primarily, by teachers' sense of purpose, by their attitudes toward students, by their interpersonal competence, and by their concern for learner well-being. Some practitioners work zealously, without diminishing their standards, to develop security and contentment in their students. Others in contrast, seem committed to the notion that children were meant to dislike school and suffering is a fundamental convenant of the educational process.

One of the peculiarities of education is that children are rarely noncommittal about their schoolhouse experiences. They either enjoy their classes or they don't, and they form definite impressions as to whether or not they are liked by their teachers. The number of children who feel that teachers are natural enemies is staggering; often a child believes that his teacher expects the worst of him, relishes assigning low grades, and takes special satisfaction in punishing. These impressions may be wrong, but the students nonetheless behave as if they were right. In the communion between student and teacher, rapport is a powerful force. Upon occasion, admittedly, an irreconcilable personality clash develops between a child and a teacher. As in adult relationships, some couplings simply were never meant to be. Still, master teachers are generally able to fathom the inner workings of students who do not fit in easily, to make adjustments, and ultimately to win cooperation through supportive gestures.

Learners, moreover, are remarkably adept at judging the extent of a teacher's compassion, interest in teaching, fondness for students, and basic human warmth. These qualities are reflected in the rules teachers make, the means by which they are enforced, and the spirit they manifest. The young, it hardly needs saying, have an ingrained predilection for mischief and, at times, a capricious need to rebel against authority. Allowed to get out of hand, or even exaggerated, such inclinations can be disastrous. Some teachers, in fact, literally are driven from the profession by the stresses they create.

Yet, many teachers have classes that take no special delight in being a nuisance. Principals have long marveled at the way students alter their demeanor from teacher to teacher: a child can be a terror with one teacher at nine A.M. and a model of decorum with another an hour later. In healthy classrooms some good-natured teasing and skirmishing may go on, and a bit of time-honored jousting occurs from time to time, but underneath there lies a friendship and a mutual interest in cooperation. There are, in sum, teachers whom children love and those whom they do not.

The girl glared malevolently at the vice-principal as she handed her the note from the teacher. Silently, the vice-principal read the message:

Dear June:

Sorry to bother you with Rosie. She broke one of our classroom rules, and when I objected, she called me—audibly—an ''old fart.''

My primary annoyance, I might add, comes from being called "old."

Actually, I'm rather fond of Rosie. Her language, I suspect, reflected her customary means of expression, and was triggered by some personal upset, but, still, I can't condone rule infractions. She's bright; a good student when she wants to be; and something of a natural leader. There's no need, I think, to be particularly tough on her.

The vice-principal looked up, glanced at the girl, and said matter-of-factly: "I'll have to assign you a detention, Rosie."

"He sure hates me," the girl said bitterly.

"What makes you think that?"

"He's always dumping on me for something or other."

The vice-principal looked steadily at the girl. "Actually," she said quietly, "he really likes you."

"Sure," the girl responded sarcastically.

The administrator handed Rosie the teacher's note. When the girl looked at her inquiringly, the older woman said: "Read it."

Rosie read the note, chewed her lip thoughtfully, and said nothing. But it was the last time she ever was sent to the office.

Children are not asked whether they want to attend school. They go, sometimes willingly and sometimes unwillingly, because they are compelled to do so by law. Many therefore regard formal education as an obligation. Older students may see a connection between schooling and a good job, but younger ones are impelled chiefly by the hope that they will find some source of gratification. Hence, when formal learning has some sort of allure, a tremendous advantage is obtained.

It is mainly atmosphere and mood, and not subject, that determine whether the classroom is a place the student wants to be. It does not matter, particularly, whether the rules are stringent or lax, whether the work is rigorous or easy, or whether the teacher is flamboyant or restrained: a classroom exhibiting all of these characteristics can be inviting or uninviting.

Mood and atmosphere (*aura*, perhaps, is a better word) can be facilitated, but not assured. That is, various kinds of teaching techniques can be used which, although useful in promoting effective learning, do not affect the basic quality of the classroom temper. Therefore, in our experimental training efforts, we talked about the virtues of a relaxed manner and periodic informality, the benefits of class "celebrations" when some special goal was reached, the occasional foregoing of homework, now and then, as a surprise treat. We also stressed—again and again—the advantages of making the classroom a pleasant place to be. We explored legitimate devices through which learning could be made more pleasurable, teaching procedures that convert the child's natural desire for play into profitable learning, and the communication of teacher dedication through verbal and nonverbal acts.

In advocating an enticing classroom atmosphere and a caring teacher, there was no insistence upon specific approaches, particular teaching styles, or any given set of academic standards. It was suggested, in fact, that when things go right in the classroom, very high expectations, in the way of student achievement, can prevail. In a marvelous line of Montaigne's from "Of the Education of Boys," he observes that "there is nothing like alluring the appetite and affections: else we shall produce only asses laden with books."

The word *love*, in recent time, has become something of a shibboleth—often misconstrued and frequently abused. It was used in conjunction with the experiments, nevertheless, because it was a popular term of the moment and because it approximated what I had in mind with respect to teacher solicitude and concern. Great teachers frequently make a deliberate effort to demonstrate—for each student—tangible signs of interest and affection. A good deal of attention, therefore, was devoted to illustrating "caring attitudes" and classroom practices that permit the teacher to show a personal investment in the individual learner. A number of strategies can be used to provide, periodically, a few moments with each student on a one-to-one basis. During these meetings the teacher can learn more about the students' idiosyncrasies, probe more deeply into their feelings about school, detect latent or active anxieties, and—of greatest importance—demonstrate friendship.

There are those, admittedly, who disparage the idea of classroom mood. Contending that the atmosphere of a classroom has little to do with student performance, they prefer to emphasize the hard core of teaching technology, the specific behaviors through which teachers explain, review, and summarize. For them, the educational process is defiled whenever it deviates from tested procedures and a strict adherence to rigorous practice. Anything designed to appeal, to engage the senses, or to draw the mind is so much wasted motion.

Children, though, are deferential to their emotions. They participate willingly, even eagerly, when they like what is going on, and only reluctantly when they are forced into activities which stultify the spirit. Thus a receptive learner makes an enormous difference. It has been said, in fact, that when youngsters want to acquire knowledge, it is almost impossible to teach a class so badly that they do not learn. Conversely, angry, hostile, uncooperative children may refuse to learn, no matter how well they are taught.

What children do, whenever they can, is play. Much of their early learning, in fact, is embedded in play. Even during adolescence, however, receptivity increases when learning has a sportive element. In all intellectual endeavor, there is a fusion between the playful and the formal—between satisfying the human need for amusement and accomplishing the task at hand. Play is reflected in Picasso's whimsy, in Haydn's musical jokes, in Shakespeare's puns. Rather than diminish achievement, play, in the right balance, can enrich work and lend vitality to labor.

The chief difficulty is that, too often, means and ends are confused: the play becomes dominant and learning suffers. Thus it is not an appealing classroom atmosphere which should be avoided, but rather excesses committed in the name of atmosphere—a preoccupation with artificially contrived experiences which distort the goals of instruction. During the humanistic splurge of the sixties and early seventies, for example, it was this kind of exaggeration that often created havoc. Rigorous student effort and skillful teaching can both occur in classroom settings where the environment is congenial.

A good classroom is neither permissive nor oppressive. Although the teacher clearly is in control and is respected by the students, an aura of solicitude exists. When the teacher, at times, is dictatorial, it is a benevolent dictatorship. And when the pupils, advertently or inadvertently, slip beyond reasonable bounds of behavior, they are easily brought back—either because of their desire to please their teacher, their interest in learning, their acceptance of necessary decorum, or all three. While learning is taken as a serious business, there is room for occasional levity, banter, and an enjoyment of the humor which so often arises in the process of learning.[1]

Above all, there is an abundant feeling of good will. Artist teachers are exceedingly sensitive to the well-being of their pupils. Blessed with sure perception, they anticipate and forestall problems before they are full-born. Sensing that an insecure child is about to do something silly to gain attention, they create an errand so that the attention comes before an untoward incident materializes. Rather than allowing a notoriously lackadaisical student to miss a deadline, they anticipate the problem, and by coaxing, spurring, or cajoling drag the assignment out of the student in good time, thus sparing the youngster a penalty. Recognizing the sure signs of boredom about to engulf a quick learner, they manage to wander by at exactly the right moment to suggest an additional elaboration in the work, and the dying interest is suddenly given new life. Classroom mood, in short, is not an act of nature: it is highly responsive to the manipulations of the teacher.

Once the participants found that the ambiance of the learning environment could be maneuvered and saw virtue in such maneuvering, they became quite skillful. They devised procedures for "reading class pulse" (judging the learners' attitudes toward the ongoing activity), anticipating impending "turn-off" (detecting progressive disinterest in the lesson), "shifting gears" (recognizing when to terminate an activity), and "injecting stimuli" (making calculated use of extemporaneous tests, wagers, mock competition). Anticipation is of consummate importance in managing a class. The teacher who can recognize early warning signals is able to make readjustments before problems reach crisis proportions. On the other hand the one who misses these signals often is in the position of being too late with too little. Quick and accurate perception, in fact, proved so important that several auxiliary exercises, described in Chapter 12, were added to the experimental framework.

One interesting outcome of the experiments had to do with enlisting the help of the students. Many teachers were adept at detecting disintegrating morale. By observing their students closely, they could sense, relatively early, mounting student tension and unease. They were unable to correct matters, however, without sacrificing momentum. The only way to counter student fatigue, seemingly, involved bringing the learning exercise to a halt and shifting to a more appealing activity. But they were reluctant to lower their goals and settle for a slower rate of achievement. Frustrated, many hit upon the simple solution of asking their classes, directly, what would help. In a surprising number of situations, the students themselves were able to suggest alternatives which helped considerably. Perhaps they had a desire to make their own advice work, but they nevertheless were able to come up with a number of insightful ideas. There is much to indicate, in fact, that students—naturally given to making up games—can invent learning activities which are both fun and productive.

Martha Adcock teaches the eighth grade in Chicago. Now in her tenth year of teaching, she works in a school with a large percentage of ethnic minority children. One of nine teachers on her faculty who participated in the artistry experiment, she was, from the very start, one of its most enthusiastic supporters. Yet—her great interest notwithstanding—she met with little early success.

In her first attempt at a device that would make the classwork more appealing, she asked the students to draw something, during the art period, that they had learned in science. Needless to say, the gambit met with a singular lack of success. Her next endeavor was even less successful: she divided the class into panels and assigned each a topic for discussion. Dismayed by the second failure, she did nothing for a few weeks but then, as her courage returned, she tried again by offering a Friday prize to students who did not receive any behavior checks during the week. Again nothing was accomplished. Most teachers, at this point, would have given the whole thing up. Still undaunted, however, Martha persisted.

Her determination was all the more surprising because the school environment was predominantly negative. In a faculty of twenty-three only nine chose to participate. Moreover, several of those uninvolved were not only skeptical but, upon occasion, even derisive. The principal, supportive in the beginning, lost interest as other, more pressing matters required attention. And, finally, the school was hampered by poor morale: Students were accustomed to repressive controls and boredom. Undeterred by these assorted obstacles, Martha continued her efforts. She was driven, apparently, by the conviction that her school—more than most—was desperately in need of instructional revitalization.

Her faith, happily, was rewarded: after another false start or two she hit the jackpot! Trying to convey the essence of barter to her yawning clients, she was seized by a visionary notion. She asked each student to bring some small unwanted object from home for a "trading" session the following day. Allowing the class fifteen minutes to bargain, she watched in amazement as the students haggled with keen intensity. At the conclusion of the trading, those who felt they had made a poor deal immediately demanded another opportunity. Obligingly, Martha scheduled a second "barter time" for the next week.

The following semester, Martha Adcock organized a comprehensive unit on trade. Using the barter sessions as a vehicle, she incorporated five substantive concepts: (1) people buy, sell, and exchange commodities, (2) money is both a medium of exchange and a measure of value, (3) barter involves the exchange of goods, wares, and labor without transfer of money, (4) material value is influenced by human desire, and (5) nations trade in much the same fashion as individuals.

Persistence, it would seem, has its own virtue in the pursuit of artistry.

12

LESSON STAGING

The teacher entered the eighth-grade science classroom a few moments after the bell had rung. He carried a hammer, a yardstick, and a newspaper. Looking briefly at the class, he said, ''Let's begin with a simple experiment today.''

Stepping in front of his desk, he carefully centered the yardstick so that half of it was suspended in the air, extending outward toward the students, and the other half was balanced on the desk. Then, standing beside the suspended half of the yardstick, he grasped the hammer, raised it high, preparing to strike the unsupported end.

The hammer began to descend in a furious stroke, but, midway, he abruptly jerked back his arm, looking intently at the boys in the first row, who, although fascinated, held their arms up protectively in anticipation of a yardstick that would suddenly fly across the room.

''What's going to happen?'' the teacher asked. ''Why are your hands up?''

''The yardstick could hit us!'' a boy exclaimed.

''No way,'' the teacher responded. ''It will break in half.''

The teacher again raised the hammer high, glanced at the students in the first row, observed that their hands again were guarding their faces, paused reflectively, and abruptly lowered the hammer.

''You might just be right,'' he said thoughtfully. Gazing about the room for a moment he asked: ''Suppose I really want to hit this yardstick just to see what happens. How can I make sure that no one gets hit?''

The students were silent at first, and then several absurd suggestions were jokingly offered. Finally, someone said: "You could put a weight over the part of the yardstick on the desk; then it won't fly out when you hit it."

"Not bad," the teacher responded. "Let's try it."

He looked around the room thoughtfully and finally called the largest boy in the class. Following the teacher's direction, the heavy lad climbed on the desk and planted both feet firmly on the yardstick. The teacher again returned to the front of the desk, raised the hammer, looked at the students, and smiled when he saw that the first row of students now had their hands down.

The teacher started to bring the hammer down and, midway, again interrupted his swing. Turning to the class, he said: "This really isn't a very nice thing to do; it's kind of mean to make Joey stand on the desk just because he's the largest student in the room. Go on back to your seat, Joey," he directed.

The teacher then laid the hammer aside and, with a few deliberate movements, covered the entire surface of the desk with a single thickness of newspaper. Picking up the hammer, he returned to the front of the desk, raised it high, and, one more time, looked at the first row. The students' hands were up.

"What's going to happen?" the teacher asked.

"It will break through the paper," a student said quickly. "Put Joey back up there."

"I don't think so," the teacher said, "but let's see."

He brought the hammer high above his head, once more acting as if he intended to strike the yardstick, then, casually glancing at the clock, he exclaimed: "Wow! I've lost track of the time. There are only a few minutes left, and I've got to review Friday's test." Without further ado, the teacher abruptly pushed all of the paraphernalia aside.

"Hit it, hit it!" several students shouted.

Ignoring these entreaties, the teacher calmly opened the text and began reviewing the forthcoming test.

The next day, when class convened, there were immediate questions. Several students, the night before, had taken a yardstick, balanced it on a table top or television set, covered the surface with a newspaper, and struck the yardstick with a hammer. How, they wanted to know, could the newspaper reduce the momentum so much?

The teacher then delivered a technical explanation of area pressure.

The maneuvers in our third set of experiments that we eventually came to call "staging" perhaps contributed more directly to improved teacher performance than any of the other experimental procedures. The term was used to identify those strategies through which teachers direct, or stage, student learning. In its technical sense, staging has to do with process—with the various devices a teacher uses to accomplish his or her purpose. If the objective is, say, to explain the principle of friction, an almost limitless variety of tactics are available. Students can be asked to read the text, listen to a lecture, observe a classroom demonstration, test a hypothesis, watch a film presentation, or work with an auto-instructional program. To assess student understanding, the teacher can assign an essay, give a test, or ask the students to discover several everyday examples of friction. Or the class can be required to determine whether powder or flour is more effective in reducing friction. Staging is that aspect of artistry with which gifted teachers reduce student apathy through absorbing assignments.

Lee DeVito teaches fifth grade in a small town in rural Illinois. A first-year teacher, Lee formerly worked for eight years as a section manager in a department store. Now, after eight months of teaching, he is reasonably content. He likes his students, gets along with his colleagues and administrators, and takes satisfaction in his conviction that helping children learn is a more worthwhile way to spend one's life than managing the television department of a store.

Somewhat traditional in his approach to teaching, his major fear is that he is not "giving the kids enough." He is also concerned about his communication skills: periodically he has a disquieting feeling that he is "talking over the kids' heads." His methods, for the most part, are conservative, both because of his cautious nature and because he was warned during his training to rely upon established procedures.

Although not particularly attracted to the artistry experiments, he agreed to participate since the other upper primary teachers chose to become involved. Without an especially colorful personality, but systematic in attention to detail and careful in decision making, Lee DeVito found staging devices the most appealing of the four theater metaphors.

Despite his lack of flamboyance, Lee had a knack for judging whether or not a teaching device would work. In his first effort at extending artistry, he devised a game that demonstrated multiple word meanings and sentence context. Any student could, as an extra activity, select any word, use it in a sentence, and define its meaning. For example, one student chose to use "bill" in "The grocer submitted his bill." Five points were given for a word used in this way. Then another student could look for an alternative usage of the word and use it in a different sentence: "The Congressman introduced a new bill." Second-meaning sentences were awarded ten points. Others then had the right to search out a third usage: "The play bill was printed on white paper." Third-meaning sentences earned twenty points. The contrivance achieved its purpose: Mr. DeVito's students not only responded to the competitive challenge, but also developed a growing fascination with the diversity of word meanings.

His second effort was tied to a geography unit. Frustrated by the class's inability to grasp the workings of latitude and longitude, he had the inspired idea of plotting the classroom itself: rows were represented as longitudes and seats as latitudes. Thus, with the room divided into a grid, the students were able to identify various objects—their seats, the teacher's desk, the wastebasket—by latitude and longitude. This device, too, was successful: the class quickly grasped the concept of a meridian reference point in relation to direction; they enjoyed pinpointing the exact location of room objects; and Mr. DeVito was able to proceed further into the unit.

In his third innovation, he decided to do something about classroom atmosphere. While there were no difficulties to speak of, he felt that student enthusiasm could be enhanced. After rejecting several other possibilities, he launched the "Question of the Day."

Again focusing on geography, the subject which seemed least appealing to his class, he assigned each student a specific calendar date in the month, since there were exactly thirty students in the class. On the assigned day, the student read a question he or she had prepared: "What country leads the world in wheat production?" "How long is the Panama Canal?" "Does it snow in the Canary Islands?" Using the classroom resource materials, other members of the class then set about finding the correct answer as quickly as possible. The student discovering the correct answer first was given a candy bar. (After some prompting from anxious mothers, a nutritional bar was substituted for the candy.) Once again, Mr. DeVito was successful: the child who made up the question spent a little extra time with books; the class's ability to use research and reference materials increased steadily; and, not insignificantly, the children accumulated an impressive collection of geographical facts.

Mr. DeVito's inventions were, of course, imaginative. In talking with him, however, I was most struck with his seemingly uncanny ability to pick winners. When I asked him what the secret was, he shrugged and said, "You just ask yourself whether the kids will like it." Part of his aptitude, clearly, lay in the ability to think not just as an adult, but also as a fifth grader.

In dealing with staging the teachers were again urged to stay within the bounds of accepted canons of teaching and learning and to devise techniques that would increase the dramatic appeal of their conventional lessons. Out of the conviction that creative impulse is stimulated by a genuine belief in the value of a technique, various methods for reducing student apathy and boredom were demonstrated. Thereafter, teachers were simply asked to invent similar devices of their own relevant to their particular teaching situation. In time, most became convinced that effective staging procedures can be used to pique children's curiosity, help maintain classroom order, reinforce cognitive concepts, draw out shy students, and encourage a receptive attitude toward the subject matter.

Staging suggests an arranging of classroom events to achieve a desired effect. It implies, in the metaphor of the theater alluded to earlier, that the teacher must at various times serve as playwright, director, and producer. Teaching involves far more than telling. To learn, a child must grasp an idea, internalize it, incorporate it with previous knowledge, and understand how to use it at appropriate times, in appropriate ways. For these things to happen the child must listen, question, practice, and apply the idea. Such requirements are the targets toward which teachers aim their staging. Because the student must listen, teachers try to make their explanations intriguing; since the learner must question in order to clarify meaning, they create tasks which necessitate inquiry; inasmuch as the student must practice, they invent drills that have an element of fun; and because the learner must apply, they assign practical problems to be solved.

A good deal of dramatic interest, in fact, can be engendered through the invention of interesting ways to use acquired knowledge. Particularly where the teacher's mission is to increase skill through repeated practice, a novel and imaginative exercise can do much to dissipate student fatigue: arithmetic can be used in conjunction with opinion polls; historical situations can be compared with present events; grammatical construction can be practiced in letters to newspaper editors or to people students admire.

In any given teaching episode, moreover, a variety of objectives are possible. A master teacher, in fact, will often have what might be called minor goals, major goals, and super goals in mind when organizing a classroom activity. The teacher may, for example, wish to improve the class's ability to engage in intellectual discourse (minor goal), help the students grasp the relationship between inflation and unemployment (major goal), and, at the same time, instill a value regarding society's obligation to provide jobs for those who wish to work (super goal). The likelihood of accomplishing these goals can be increased substantially through skillful staging. Specific maneuvers, for example, can be used to highlight the discrete elements of the lesson and to ensure that each has taken root. Every staging tactic, to be pedagogically justifiable, must have a point: the learners must see the connection between the lure, so to speak, and the goal. When multiple objectives are intended, consequently, different staging strategies are a considerable help in drawing attention to the separate aims.

There is another interesting side effect of staging. Virtually every practitioner is, at times, dispirited by frustration. Often, for example, vital elements of the curriculum may have little appeal for some students. Such content nonetheless must be taught. A teacher who is obliged to teach seemingly vapid material to unwilling learners cannot help but be disaffected. Even the most dedicated sometimes limit the energy they invest in classroom work which is wearisome to their learners. In such circumstances teachers function at a level well below their potential.

Staging can help to counteract both student disinterest and instructor frustration in two distinct ways. First, an imaginative attempt to increase student interest—by dramatizing the special quality of a topic—is in itself an energizing professional challenge; and second, when the challenge is met; and a class's

attention awakened, a major source of teacher frustration is removed. Many of our experiments, consequently, were devoted to
discovering and exploiting the hidden, and frequently unsuspected,
attraction of a study unit. Ways were found, for example, to teach
the laws of chemistry through an examination of cosmetic prepara-
tions, the principles of musical form through record albums by the
Beatles, the economics of supply and demand through homework
assignments involving barter, and the power of poetic expression
through analyses of advertising slogans.

Artistry in staging converges around the practitioner's dexterity in
organizing and directing learning exercises. The genesis of this kind of
deftness stems from imagination, creativity, desire, and a consummate understanding of both subject and learner. Certain individuals,
for example, are admired for their ability to give lively and interesting
parties. Their skill stems not merely from the ''logic'' that enables
them to choose a tasteful menu, but also from an intuitive sense about
a good mix of people, an ability to create an appropriate ambiance,
and a flair for initiating conversation that the guests find provocative.
Some clergymen, through extra effort, seem to go beyond the routine
demands of their ministry and create among their parishioners feelings of camaraderie, rapport, and identity. Their success in this regard
derives not from brilliant sermons or compassionate pastoral counseling, but rather from adeptness in promoting a group spirit. Similarly,
many teachers—who are neither extraordinary scholars nor blessed
with spectacular ''color''— nonetheless achieve exciting classrooms.
The things that go on in these classrooms are intriguing to the students. Although solid learning occurs, the activities seem more like
play than work. There is, after all, nothing cheap about baiting learner
interest; only cheap bait is cheap. The classroom drama can be staged
with sensitivity, high style, and finesse. Such teachers recognize that
intellectual effervescence is both more instructive and more pleasant
than intellectual languor.

Danielle Ryan has a natural gift for teaching. When I proposed
the artistry experiment to her principal, she exclaimed: ''We have
one like that! Everyone admires her cleverness; the other
teachers use her ideas all the time.''
Mrs. Ryan is indeed good. Bright and knowledgeable, she
teaches with a driving energy. Constantly in motion, she smiles at

one child, frowns at another, and shakes her fist in mock threat at two boys giggling over some piece of silliness, as she walks rapidly from group to group. The real yeast of her artistry, however, is in her ability to awaken dormant capacities. "They learn so much more quickly," she said to me, "when they want to. You've got to get all their resources going. Otherwise, they just go through the motions."

On my first visit to her room, a box was drawn in the upper-left-hand corner of the chalkboard. There was a permanent caption, in colored chalk: "Today's Teaser." Underneath was a cryptic question: "Do they have a Fourth of July in England?" On my second visit, the daily "teaser" read: "If your doctor gave you three pills and said to take one every half hour, how long would they last?" And when I observed a third time, the question was: "How many birthdays does the average woman have?"

Watching her lead a discussion on Japan, I was startled—after she questioned one child and received an answer—to hear her say: "Paraphrase, please, Tina." A second child immediately restated, in her own words, the answer given by the previous student. Later, I asked Danielle the purpose of such repetitions. "Several reasons," she replied. "First, by having the kids paraphrase each other's answers, I can check the understanding of two at the same time. Second, they have to keep on their toes because they don't know who will be called upon for the paraphrasing. Third, they really need to listen to one another in order to sort out the significant points. And fourth, I have a double opportunity to clarify misconceptions."

When I was in her room on another occasion, I could not help but notice envelopes at each child's place. The youngsters were reading a story, and—as they finished—they opened the envelopes and studied five slips of paper intently. Each child then sorted the slips in a particular pattern. Curious, I asked Mrs. Ryan what was going on. " After they finish the story," she explained, "they have to arrange the events, written on the slips, in the order of occurrence. It helps them read carefully and remember sequence," she added.

Teachers like Danielle are blesed with great natural aptitude. They take advantage of possibilities that the rest of us overlook. But they also are energized by a passion to succeed. As with stellar athletes and musical virtuosos, talent and commitment together produce exceptional performance.

EPILOGUE

The characteristics associated with artistry come readily to mind—skill, originality, flair, dexterity, ingenuity, virtuosity, and similar qualities which, together, engender exceptional performance. These, clearly, contribute to the aesthetics of pedagogy. Artistry also consists of master craftsmanship through which tasks are conceived, planned, and executed with unusual imagination and brilliance. Or to approach the phenomenon from yet another perspective, it could be said that artistry stems from the subtle discrimination and judgment which come from extraordinary perception. Regardless of the descriptive terms used, however, artistry implies teaching that is unusual in its proficiency and greatly superior to conventional practice.

Artistry involves attitudes as well as intentions, knowledge coupled with discernment, and uncommon deftness. These, moreover, must together form a cohesive force: great skill wasted on trivial objectives, virtuous aims pursued unimaginatively, and ingenious tactics executed poorly—all defeat artistry. In teaching, excellence involves (a) choosing instructional objectives that have high worth, (b) using imaginative and adroit ways to achieve these objectives, and (c) attacking the objectives with great skill and dexterity. The cultivation of artistry, consequently, requires that teachers develop a perceptive sense of purpose, exploit their capacity for creative invention in accomplishing this purpose, and acquire a corresponding repertory of technical skills.

These, in addition, must be conjoined in a nexus—a framework—that fits the classroom setting, the temper of the students, and the demands of reality. It is senseless, for example, to choose objectives that ignore public expectation, to devise teaching gambits which are unsuited to the learners, or to use instructional strategies which run counter to the school's aspirations. Sensibility, in a word, is crucial.

As this book was in the final stages of completion, a spate of national reports calling for major educational reform appeared. The commentary reflected rising concern over the nation's seeming inability to compete in international markets, alarm over falling test scores, and a pervasive suspicion that American education had grown soft in the center. The rhetoric hammered, again and again, at three basic messages: First, "the nation is at risk" because competitors are overtaking America's once unchallenged lead in industry, science, and technology. Second, ineptness has become the norm in American education; a "rising tide of mediocrity" endangers the educational foundations of our society. The poor performance of our students on international achievement tests, the increasing illiteracy rate, the decline in Scholastic Aptitude Test scores, and the growing need for remedial instruction—all testify to the low ebb we have reached. Third, though alarming, these conditions are not beyond repair. Historically, when it becomes evident that education is in need of renovation, major improvements are initiated. We are now, once again, at a crisis point and drastic changes are required. Yet, Ernest Boyer, in reflecting upon these recommendations, stresses that "whatever is wrong with America's public schools cannot be fixed without the help of those teachers already in the classrooms."[1]

The reports call for lengthening the school day and year, shifting the ages of compulsory education, putting more emphasis on academics, providing additional instruction in science and mathematics, developing computer literacy, tightening discipline, raising standards, allowing tuition tax credits and tuition vouchers, requiring study of a foreign language, adopting harder textbooks, eliminating tracking, and awarding merit pay to teachers to encourage better teaching. It is the last of these that is particular relevent to artistry in the classroom.

[handwritten marginal note: responding to Sig't'r Nat. @ Risk]

While the reports failed to define good teaching, they did recommend rigorous assessment of teacher competence. Such evaluation, obviously, necessitates agreement on the knowledge and skills teachers should have, as well as on criteria for judging teacher effectiveness. Consensus, needless to say, is not easily reached. Opinions differ considerably with respect to the school's primary mission, the relative importance of different instructional goals, and the role of teachers.

Moreover, we are far from expert at measuring teaching skill and overall student learning. Good classroom results, as we have seen, are brought about in various ways. There are, furthermore, no guaranteed procedures, either in the training of teachers or in the teaching of students. Because instructional conditions vary, different things work in different places. Thus, if we were foolish enough to specify exactly what teachers should and should not do, we would constrict the full range of a teacher's potential.

Cause and effect in teaching, it might be added, are anything but certain. The relationship between what a teacher does and the resulting consequences is not fixed. On the surface, for example, a teacher's failure to answer a question would seem to be an instructional error. Sometimes, however, skilled teachers provoke independent learning by requiring their youngsters to puzzle things out for themselves. Mortimer Adler in his *Paideia* points out, for example, that the teacher's role is to aid students in the process of discovery.[2]

Logically, it would be sensible to (a) select instructional aims, (b) prescribe appropriate methods for achieving these aims, and (c) determine whether they have been reached. But in the welter of classroom occurrences such organizational tidiness is often impossible. Even if the same objectives were desirable in every situation, special goals can be of particular importance in an unusual circumstance. On occasion, for example, it may be better to disregard a mistake temporarily in order to build a student's confidence. Similarly, mathematics teachers might correct spelling errors, an English instructor teach a bit of related history, or an athletic coach encourage a halfback to read a current novel.

Artist teachers abandon convention and pursue something off-beat. Music instructors, in teaching a child to play the trumpet, generally model the correct position of the lips. When, however, a student is unable to "feel" the correct *embouchure*, the teacher may ask the child to place a piece of paper against a wall and, by directing a steady stream of air against its center, keep it from falling. Artist teachers, in fact, excel at such impromptu contrivances when the conventional method doesn't seem to work.

Teaching, in the richest sense of the art, is far more than rule-following. It is tempting to assume that if an instructor knows what to do, when and how it should be done, and follows procedure, uniformly excellent results will be obtained. Unfortunately, however, standardized practices only go so far. Picasso, after all, did not paint by the numbers. Given a choice between two teachers—one with a good command of methods and the other with an ability to motivate learners—most principals would instinctively choose the motivator. There are times, in fact, when pedagogical laws can be broken to good advantage.

The best teachers, as earlier chapters suggested, exercise a considerable amount of personal judgment. They yield to their instincts, make use of their intuitive powers, improvise when necessary, and generally approach teaching with an open mind. And, in their efforts to be more effective, they frequently turn to the novel and untried. Such teachers would undoubtedly lose their enthusiasm, fire, and wizardry if required to follow a prescribed formula. Rules and prescriptions have their place. They serve as a guide for neophytes and as a point of departure for those more experienced. The routinization of teaching, nonetheless, would do more harm than good.

Artist teachers—whether they use conventional or unconventional methods—must be free to do things better. They are set apart, in this regard, much as Albert Einstein, Galileo, Harriet Tubman, and Beethoven stood above other performers in their respective fields. Artistry, in short, is more than spontaneity and invention, inspiration and motivation, dramatization and a colorful personality: it is an extraordinary level of performance, bred out of personal commitment, which elevates the state of the art.

Other "logical" assumptions about the improvement of teaching implied in the reports are equally troublesome. There is not, for example, and exact connection between a teacher's actions and the amount of learning that occurs. The appeal of the subject matter, the enthusiasm of the students, the time of day, and a host of other factors affect achievement. For example, the quality of the instructional materials, the aptitude of the students, the number of classroom interruptions, the extent of parent reinforcement in homework—and similar elements beyond the teacher's control—also influence the outcome of instruction. As a result, it is virtually impossible to plan teaching completely in advance, one unpredictability or another alters the situation. Thus, adaptability—the capacity to compensate for unforeseen difficulties—is a significant benchmark of excellence. Teachers who year after year get excellent results are distinguished by their ability to cope: to modify one thing or another and circumvent problems. This, in the main, is why training institutions, supervisors, and principals cannot dictate teacher behavior according to code. Possibilities can be suggested, the "tricks of the pedagogue" can be described, and vision expanded—but, in the last analysis, an ability to accommodate the unforeseen is critical.

One further misconception abounds: the presumption that instructors are uniformly good or bad in all situations. Most teachers are better at one facet of teaching than another. Some may be most effective with bright youngsters; others relate well to slow learners. While one is wonderfully adept at clarifying misunderstandings, another has a rare ability to challenge students' minds through skillful questions. Some work best with small groups, some with large, and many are superb in one-to-one situations. Often, therefore, a teacher's effectiveness depends upon the luck of the draw—an assignment that happens to fit individual strengths. There are, in sum, various kinds of expert teaching.

The question that teachers invariably ask is, "What can I do that will make me more artistic?" The answer frequently is received with disappointment. Desire, persistent effort, and imagination do not come in three simple steps. The case studies of artist teachers reveal specific actions, but they are the secondary effects of a fundamental mind-set. This, perhaps, helps explain why artistry exists in different forms.

The roots of great teaching lie in attitude, ideology, dedication, and passion. Raw talent is not enough. Many who have the potential for artistry fall short of the mark. The problem is not the lack of ability but rather the absence of professional "hunger." Those who seek a simple path to excellence are disappointed because—although we can show them gadgetry, tricks, razzle-dazzle devices, and clever maneuvers—all of these are the symbols, not the source, of artistry. The real genesis, as we have seen, is an abiding personal devotion to the art of teaching. Without such devotion, ordinary teachers may use skillful artistic procedures, but the end result is not authentic artistry. Hence, formula and rule have but limited utility.

A comparison of the following two profiles makes the point:

Gloria has been teaching for eighteen years. Early in her career, she commonly worked twelve to fourteen hours a day. Now, ten hours usually suffice. As a beginning teacher, most of her work time at home was devoted to preparation. As her expertness increased she began using the time differently, spending more and more of it analyzing her children's written assignments. The daughter of a school superintendent, she has an uncompromising distaste for mediocrity. Home, classroom, dress—and teaching—reflect an unmistakable penchant for quality. Thoroughness, excellence, and "going the extra mile," she believes, are important.

She also thinks a bit of anxiety is good for kids, particularly brighter ones. Able learners, she says, who usually have too easy a time, need lots of challenge and push. Recently, one of her seven-year-olds wrote a book. A collection of short stories—about moving from one city to another—were joined together. The child designed her own cover and the teacher provided the binding. Gloria places heavy emphasis on organization and structure. At the start of each semester she spends a considerable amount of time teaching her students how they are to behave, where things belong, and what they are to do. The kids must learn to function alone so that she is free to work with particular groups. What she calls "routines"—systems for avoiding interruptions and unnecessary complications—are crucial. The children obtain materials, sharpen pencils, and move to work centers in designated ways. A child who needs help does not call out or ask for attention. Instead, a "red flag"—folded cardboard tied to a stick—is raised, and Gloria comes to the student as soon as she can. Classroom discipline, needless to say, is not a problem. To teach well, she maintains, a teacher must have as much "quality time" with individuals and groups as possible. Her classes quickly learn to read the nonverbal signals she sends as she moves from task to task: an uplifted eyebrow for a rule infraction, a pointed finger for unnecessary chatting, a penetrating stare when someone is not concentrating, and a beaming smile when the kids catch on.

Other teachers dismay her. She avoids the lunchroom and almost never goes to the faculty lounge. At noon, she needs some "private space" and quiet. Moreover, she says, the conversation topics in the faculty lounge are invariably boring. Exchanging war stories about what the kids did and rehashing last night's TV programs holds no charm for her. The joy in teaching, she feels, comes from watching children develop intellectually.

Gloria believes the schools should be reorganized and that teacher training, especially, should be revitalized. More observation time should be spent in good classrooms, and the lecture-hall theory should be tied to the teaching going on in children's classrooms. Good teachers are personally motivated, persistent, and interested in their kids. She advises the student teacher with whom she works to "get there early and make sure things are ready, question what you do and why, be well read, learn to pick the right questions to ask, find a good control system that you like, pay lots of attention to the little touches, and keep learning."

Cindy is constantly on the lookout for good classroom activities. She is particularly interested in seat work the kids like and can do by themselves. In her eighth year of teaching, she places considerable reliance on student worksheets. "They are easy to use and get the kids ready for tests," she says. Preferring ready-made materials, she rarely creates instructional materials of her own.

She considers herself an "informal" teacher. She tends to arrive fifteen minutes before the children and is among the first to leave at the end of the day. Cindy takes pride in being well organized, primarily because she never has to take work home and always has something ready for the kids to do. Although most of the other faculty remain when specialist teachers come to their rooms to teach music or art, Cindy invariably leaves—to "relax." Her classroom rule is that the students' worksheets must be finished. When done, the children can do whatever they wish—walk around, come to the teacher's desk, or talk quietly with others—so long as those still working are not disturbed. A child who needs help may ask a neighbor or come to Cindy. When the noise level is too loud, Cindy shouts "Quiet" in a sharp voice and the din subsides.

In her early thirties, pretty, with an active social life, she views teaching as "a job." Her responsibility, she feels, is to make the sure the kids learn what they need to know to pass the tests. She sees no point in individualizing instruction and thinks teachers who become personally involved with their students are neurotic "do-gooders." "Dentists fix teeth and optometrists fit glasses," says Cindy. "Why should teachers be different? We're not psychologists or parents, we're instructors who organize children's learning. We can't learn for the kids, they have to do it."

> Reasoning this way, Cindy makes little effort to become familiar with her children's interests and problems. Although good-natured and cordial with her classes, she avoids too much involvement. For the same reasons, she takes no special joy in her students' progress.

The notion of teaching performance also can be misleading. Teachers do specific things to accomplish their goals. It is not acting, per se, nor salesmanship, nor communication, nor entertainment, nor pedagogical jugglery which account for performance. It is the *gestalt* of these—molded into a personal style, built around individual attributes, and energized by genuine commitment and an educated mind—which account for teaching that takes students beyond the confines of their interest. Artistry, as a consequence, matures over time. Fine teachers get better and better as long as the hunger for high accomplishment persists. In young teachers, natural talent may show early. True artistry, however, develops later as sustained effort and experience heighten perception, deepen judgment, and broaden pedagogical skills.

What then can be done to promote more artistic teaching, to reduce classroom instruction that lacks plot and direction, that is trifling in its intent, and a frail embodiment of good pedagogy? These, perhaps:

We can identify the characteristics of artist teachers. We can describe what they do. We can try to fathom the mysterious innuendos that direct their instincts. We can learn from what they avoid. And we can even show others how to use their maneuvers. But we cannot specify artistic behavior.

There are general principles—not laws, but principles—which help matters. Yet, in the end, every artistic coup, every imaginative stroke is forged by situational circumstances. Describing artistry heightens awareness and demonstrates new possibilities. It cannot, however, substitute for personal determination.

Artist teachers develop their own way of thinking about classroom problems, and fashion their teaching from experience. Much of their astuteness is bred from earlier mistakes. Method—for them—is the activation of simple logic. When they do things that excite interest, arouse enthusiasm, and simplify learning, they draw upon cunning acquired, not from divine insight, but from some past failure that was analyzed and thought out.

In the teacher workshops I give on artistry, there often is keen disappointment when I am unable to suggest clever artifices which can be used the next day. I argue that one does not need recipes; since one teaches anyway, there is no good reason to not work toward greater expertness. Small efforts at self-directed improvement nourish the spirit, making teaching more pleasurable, and soon produce an appreciable difference. When we take modest steps to do things a bit better, the cumulative consequences are surprisingly impressive.

It is possible, of course, to give teachers advice on the technical aspects of pedagogy. As the scholarly writings have suggested, we can demonstrate standard operating procedures,[3] convey techniques for accomplishing various tasks,[4] and show the negative consequences of bad practices,[5] but these do not produce true excellence. Artist teachers work from a far larger portfolio of skills: they organize subject matter and learning exercises efficaciously; they sense what has gone wrong in a child's thinking when comprehension stalls; they sustain the attention of the quick ones while waiting patiently for those who are slower; they discern when challenge ceases to be a stimulus and becomes a stressor; they adjust and readjust their actions to the demeanor of their students; they induce a desire to learn; they employ metaphor and analogy to enhance meaning; they strengthen minds without damaging psyches; and they open intellectual windows, exposing unsuspected views.

To do these things they must have clarity of aim and a desire to help others understand. Thousands of teachers know their subject matter, command good methods, and have effective skills. Yet they fall short of artistry. Either they do not value their craft, or they underestimate their potential, or—for all their knowledge and ability—teaching does not offer internal satisfaction. Their professional preparation failed them in these regards.

Thought, after all, cannot be separated from emotion. Hence the best training in the world will only produce slavish imitation if teachers do not grasp the full power and significance of their own creative talents. Skills, in sum, must be matched with a sense of dedication and a sense of drama. These are the true measure of training.

Artistry shows most often in the transition between aspiration and process. Once teachers focus their sights on some piece of significant learning, excellence lies in choosing the best path and following it deftly. Perpetuating artistry, therefore, necessitates collaboration within the profession. Training institutions must ensure a comprehensive general education as well as instill a love for quality; teachers themselves must become inspired; and the work setting must offer a receptive climate, support, and recognition for exceptional achievement. Too often, training is reduced to trivial mechanics: the schools tolerate mediocrity; creative imagination is fettered by bureaucratic trappings; and misguided research takes us in the wrong direction. Fine teaching, in sum, requires good preparation, devotion, and a fertile work environment.

The denigration of the art and the turn toward alien standards aside, our present system of teacher preparation is not likely to produce excellent practitioners. Not only is too much of the training devoted to conventional method and current shibboleths, but the treatment of teaching and learning is encased in doctrinaire routine, and too far removed from contemporary classroom life.

Teachers are admonished to achieve orderly schoolrooms, to prevent disruptions, to create pleasant environments, to motivate their students, and to sustain industriousness. However, they are rarely shown how to avoid problems or invent solutions. And, in many instances, their own general education is less than it should be. They learn too much, perhaps, about ancient educational philosophies and too little about the changing world. They are urged to place blind faith in the prevailing ''best way'' and to disregard their own insight and ingenuity.

During their training, teachers should have much more exposure to excellent public-school classrooms. They should receive systematic practice in developing their capacities for innovation, spontaneity, perception, and intuition. These, in the final analysis, are the yeast of artistry. They must recognize that skillful teaching grows through its own natural stages, and that every great teacher hones a natural style through continuous experimentation. They must be taught, by their mentors, that the common denominators characterizing fine teaching are the arousal of intellectual curiosity, the awakening of faculties, and the nurture of ideas. They must understand that good teaching can be formal or informal, planned or unplanned, and pursued in myriad ways:

through lecture, discussion, tutorial, example, and task. They must know that predestinate artists invariably teach themselves and find their own path. It is in thinking about teaching, while away from the chalkboard, that great ideas arise.

Two dimensions of teacher training are particularly troublesome: one has to do with analytical skills and the other with professional well-being. Most people who enter teaching are impelled, in part, by a role model, by the memory of a former teacher who was especially skillful and inspiring. Later, they are likely to discover that what was a driving force for the model is not for them. Emulation is useful, but sooner or later, every teacher must achieve a personal identity.

It was startling to find, during the experiments, that often teachers do not sense the relationship between goal and method. Some focus on the wrong aims and others choose inept techniques. Good teacher education should stress, first, ascertaining the object of a lesson, activity, or exercise, and second, comparing the diverse routes to its accomplishment. The avenues to successful teaching are many, as are the hucksters selling directions. Ultimately, however, teachers must choose their own road. No one can tell us in advance what will be best in a given situation. Student teachers should be taught simple analytical devices for determining the core idea of a concept, the key steps in acquiring a skill, the essential purpose of a drill. Once they can identify the dominant objective they should have repeated practice in experimenting with alternative strategies.

During the experiments, in one of the exercises on perception, teachers were asked to sit in on the class of a friend and observe. They were told to answer four simple questions: (1) What's happening? (2) What's good? (3) What's bad? and (4) What else could the teacher try? I was surprised by two things: their initial difficulty and their rapid improvement. Plainly told, teachers do not spend enough time, during their training, thinking about the relationship between teaching and learning.

When the teachers gathered in small groups, organized around similar interests and stylistic inclinations, they found reinforcement, freedom to risk, and security in failure. They were shown five ways to attack a learning goal and asked to invent ten more. Urged to take chances, and try things, they eventually discovered that creative teaching was less difficult than they had imagined, as well as pleasurable and productive.

The experienced teacher trainer does not begin with a preconceived notion of how teaching should proceed. Sensitive to our impoverished theory, and the sterility of conventional practice, the trainer instead studies the individual, looking for natural aptitudes and skills. The trainer teaching style is then fashioned around the student's attributes. Sharpened during professional puberty, this style takes on a distinctive shape. It organizes natural instinct and impulse, and marks the teacher's uniqueness. Some achieve their purpose through lucid talk, others through the skillful use of chalk. Those who are not particularly good at graphic arts turn, instead, to mime, or to shrewd direction and skillful planning.

Sensible teacher trainers help their students understand the technical requirements—the indispensable elements—of a well-constructed lesson, but they also press for individuality. They emphasize the need for good control, clear communication, precise aims, feedback and efficient use of time, and—at the same time—point out that all of these can be achieved in multiple ways. Just as an architect provides for the house foundation, plumbing and wiring systems, and roof support—and yet concentrates on the nature of the site and the owner's wishes—the trainer emphasizes both essentials and individuality. John Goodlad has observed that "teachers often respond eagerly to alternative methods of teaching that relate to many of their deepest professional values."[6]

Artistry comes, as much as anything else, from originality in solving teaching problems. Trainers, therefore, must not only deal with each student as a separate entity—determining what training is most suitable, capitalizing on strengths and compensating for weaknesses—but they must also unfetter and nurture the special abilities which exist. Such training—it must be said—cannot take place in the methods class. It is only through supervised practice—where the neophyte is guided by the expert—that insight, finesse, and mastery develop.

In a book of mine, published in 1978, I argued the importance of a professional coach for beginning teachers.[7] Since that time my conviction has doubled. Nothing is as important, in training teachers, as a skillful observer who knows the art and craft, who values individuality, and who excels as a sensitive mentor. It does not matter whether the coaching is done by another teacher, a supervisor, or a professor—so long as the guidance is excellent. Good coaches, it should be noted, do not work from a handbook or a collection of laws: rather, they regard every person as a special case.

We are entitled to hope, perhaps, that teaching—like painting, sculpture, and dance—will one day be viewed as an art form in which individual interpretation is prized.

At present, in a false calculus of expediency, we give student teachers rules to follow and models to copy. It doesn't work. Then, when failure is encountered, they look outward rather than inward, and search for different rules and models. What they have not learned is self-direction in finding the heart of a teaching problem, and in setting their aims correctly. They are unable to grasp the central issues, or critical skills which lead to successful learning.

If we could overcome this difficulty, it would then be possible to show student teachers the precise things which must happen before solid learning can occur. Once these are understood, they could explore—with our encouragement, goading, support, and mentoring—a variety of methods. They would thus learn why some techniques are effective, and why others are not. In time, they would themselves become skilled problem-solvers, able to teach with telling effect.

It is one thing to equate merit in teaching with outstanding results, and another to define it as "correct instruction." Much harm can occur if we fall prey to the belief that using specified methods produces masterful performance. Fixation on prescribed instructional procedures, or on rote processes, will lead to a kind of triple cloning: the teaching student must first defer to the expectations of the methods professor; then abandon these in order to placate the supervisor of student teaching; and—after professional service begins—change once again to comply with the demands of the principal. The pernicious by-product of such "right-way" doctrines is that they lead us to assume, with gullible innocence, that a master teacher can show others how to achieve excellence in a few short lessons.

It is this same preoccupation with prescriptive teaching methods which, perhaps, has contributed to the massive crisis in teacher morale. The desire to teach stems, principally, from an opportunity to accomplish things that are personally meaningful and satisfying. A teacher's style, consequently, must utilize instruction that is inherently gratifying, and that permits self-expression. Teaching abridged of human idiosyncrasy is best left to computers.

The growing penchant for pre-programmed instruction, with teaching by formula, strips away the creative impulse. It gives direction but destroys personal involvement. The result is an alienation of the professional self, disenchantment, and perfunctory performance. Teachers, like other workers who must be responsive to challenge, have a profound need to do things their own way.

Student teachers, of course, need to observe artist teachers in action, if only to become aware of what is possible. They may even need to copy a few maneuvers and imitate until their confidence and competence rise. Eventually, however, they must begin to test their own theories, find their own paths, fashion their own procedures, and draw upon the energy which stems from keen interests.

Artistry may well be the most promising antidote to the frustration, dissatisfaction, and despair which have begun to afflict many of the nation's teachers. Additional regulation in the form of mandatory methods can only result in more disillusionment, and further blunting of the imagination. It would be far better, one would think, to encourage higher expectations, greater pride in craft, and teaching behavior which is genuinely self-actuating. Without such encouragement the joys of teaching will become fewer and fewer, and the obligations of the classroom reduced to an odious chore. All artists must have a lasting love affair with their arts.

According to the Department of Labor, some fifty thousand people, each day say "I quit." Too many of these, alas, are teachers. The talented young people who leave after a year or two do so, less because of the poor pay and hard work, than because teaching was joyless, devoid of gratification, and empty of hope, incentive, and good feelings. Had they achieved that level of artistry which carries its own rewards, they might have stayed. This is the real task of teacher education; to make practitioners able enough to find genuine fulfillment in helping children learn.

A teacher's best teaching is usually the most artistic. The best teaching, moreover, is likely to occur when teachers are doing the things they enjoy. And they tend to enjoy that at which they excel. Hence, if err we must, it would be better, in teacher training, to err on the side of artistic embellishment that enables individuals to teach in ways that give pleasure, and reward.

Lastly, teacher preparation must do everything possible to rekindle idealism and to restore the glory of the mission. The times have taken a fearsome toll on educators, and many teachers and administrators are on the raw edge of despair. Disillusioned and embittered, they no longer care. There was a day—a day that must be returned—when individuals with great gifts thought the teaching of children a worthy lifetime endeavor. It still is.

NOTES

PROLOGUE

[1] Two research studies comparing the achievement of students in similar schools have found that it is important for principals to be active instructional leaders. Those schools having principals who were achievement- or task-oriented had more efficient and effective instruction. R. Venezky and L. Winfield, ''Schools that succeed beyond expectations in teaching reading,'' *Studies on Education, Technical Report Number 1* (Newark, Del.: University of Delaware, 1979); and M. Kean, A. Summers, M. Raivetz, and I. Farber, *What Works in Reading?* (School District of Philadelphia, 1979).

CHAPTER 2

[1] G. Wallace, *The Art of Thought* (New York: Harcourt, Brace and Company, 1926).

[2] J. P. Guilford, ''Three Faces of Intellect,'' *American Psychologist* 14 (1959): 469–479.

[3] More effective teachers are able to adapt their instruction to meet the needs of the errors that the students may make. This is not only true in terms of giving corrective feedback but also in providing remedial instruction in weak areas and in precorrecting potential errors before they occur. The precorrection would involve instruction specifically focused at a

potential weak or confusing concept. (B. Rosenshine and R. Stevens, *Classroom Instruction in Reading*, in press.)

CHAPTER 3

[1] Susanne Langer, *Mind: An Essay on Human Feelings*, 2 vols. (Baltimore: Johns Hopkins University Press, 1967), I: 222–228.

CHAPTER 4

[1] Robert Rosenthal, *Experimenter Effects in Behavioral Research* (New York: Irvington Publishers; distributed by Halsted Press, 1970), p. 158.

[2] James Chambliss, Excerpt from an unpublished manuscript.

[3] Charles A. Reich, *The Greening of America*. (New York: Random House, 1970), p. 131.

[4] Extracted from unpublished survey findings from American College Testing Program. Teacher expectancy has been found to influence teacher behavior, which in turn influences both pupil behavior and pupil achievement. J. P. Baker and J. L. Crist, "Teacher Expectancies: A Review of the Literature," in J. D. Elashoff and R. E. Snow, *Pygmalion Reconsidered* (Worthington, O.: Charles A. Jones, 1971), pp. 48–64.

[5] Classrooms that promote achievement gain also tend to have a strong affect focus. Those teachers develop rapport with their students and provide instruction in a warm, convivial atmosphere. N. Bennett, J. Jordan, G. Long, and B. Wade, *Teaching Style and Pupil Progress* (London: Open Books Publishing Ltd., 1976); D. Solomon and A. J. Kendall, *Children in Classrooms* (New York: Praeger, 1979).

CHAPTER 5

[1] Recent research has yielded consistent results concerning the importance of teachers as effective decision makers. The teachers who are the most successful in promoting achievement gain were also teachers who were the most effective in making instructionally relevant decisions. R. S. Soar, *Follow-Through Classroom Process Measurement and Pupil Growth, 1970–1971: Final Report* (Gainesville, Fla.: University of Florida, 1973); J. Stallings and D. Kaskowitz, *Follow-Through Classroom Observation Evaluation, 1972–1973* (Menlo Park, Calif.: Stanford Research Institute, 1974); J.

Stallings, R. Cory, J. Fairweather, and M. Needles, *Early Childhood Classroom Evaluation* (Menlo Park, Calif.: Stanford Research Institute, 1977); and D. Solomon and A. J. Kendall, *Children in Classrooms* (New York: Praeger, 1979).

[2] Jacob S. Kounin, *Discipline and Group Management in Classrooms* (New York: Holt, Rinehart and Winston, 1970).

[3] Jerome S. Bruner, Jacqueline J. Goodnow, and George A. Austin, *A Study of Thinking* (New York: John Wiley & Sons, Inc., 1956).

CHAPTER 6

[1] Although a moderate amount of anxiety can act as a motivator and facilitate high performance, high levels of anxiety can be debilitating. There is a great deal of difference among individuals in how they react to anxiety and what the optimal level of anxiety is. E. M. Gifford and A. R. Marston, "Text Anxiety, Reading Ratio and Task Experience," *Journal of Educational Research* 59 (1966): 303–306.

[2] Effective classroom management is necessary for successful classroom instruction. Studies of teachers in classrooms have emphasized the need for teachers to maintain the instructional momentum, to monitor all of the students, and to catch problems early and defuse them before they become major interruptions. J. Kounin, *Discipline and Group Management in Classrooms* (New York: Holt, Rinehart and Winston, 1970); J. Brophy and C. Evertson, *Learning from Teaching: A Developmental Perspective* (Boston: Allyn and Bacon, 1976).

CHAPTER 7

[1] From an unpublished study by Louis Rubin.

[2] J. Stallings, R. Cory, J. Fairweather, and M. Needles, *Early Childhood Classroom Evaluation* (Menlo Park, Calif.: Stanford Research Institute, 1977).

CHAPTER 8

[1] Susanne Langer, *Mind: An Essay on Human Feelings,* 2 vols. (Baltimore: Johns Hopkins University Press, 1967), 1: 222–228.

[2] Walter Kerr, "We Call It 'Live' Theater, But Is It?", New York Times, Jan. 2, 1972, p. 1:1, section 2.

[3] Kenneth Eble, *A Perfect Education* (New York: Macmillan, 1966).

[4]Eric Berne, *Games People Play* (New York: Ballantine, 1978).

CHAPTER 9

[1] A large body of research underscores the importance of maintaining students' attention during instruction. This research provides evidence of a direct relationship between the students' attention and the amount that students learn. B. Rosenshine and D. Berliner, "Academic Engaged Time," *British Journal of Teacher Education* 4 (1978) : 3–16; J. Brophy and C. Evertson, *Learning from Teaching: A Developmental Perspective* (Boston: Allyn and Bacon, 1976); and L. Anderson, "New Directions for Research on Instruction and Time-on-Task," paper presented at AERA annual meeting, Boston, April 1980.

[2] Reported in the *Wall Street Journal*, Apr. 7, 1980, p. 1, section 1 in Steven Wermiel's "A Professor Becomes the Joyce Brothers of the Legal World."

[3] One research study has found that a faster pace during the presentation of material helps to maintain students' attention. D. Carnine, "Effects of Two Teacher Presentation Rates on Off-Task Behavior, Answering Correctly and Participation," *Journal of Applied Behavior Analysis* 9(1979):100–206. Although there certainly is an upper limit on how fast the pace can be before it is detrimental, this upper limit has not been investigated. Another study trained teachers to increase their instructional pace and to hold students accountable for their work. In this study the classrooms that maintained their instructional momentum had higher student attention and high student achievement. T. Good and D. Grouws, "The Missouri Mathematics Effectiveness Project," *Journal of Educational Psychology* 7(1979):355–362.

[4] Motivational techniques are a very powerful means of getting and maintaining students' attention. This is particularly true when it comes to students' persistence at a given task. The amount of time that students are willing and able to spend on a learning task is largely related to their level of motivation. J. B. Carroll, "School Learning over the Long Haul," in J. D. Krumholtz, ed., *Learning and the Educational Process* (Chicago: Rand McNally, 1965), pp., 249–269.

CHAPTER 10

[1] Similar characteristics were exhibited by the more successful teachers in

the study done by Jacob Kounin. He found six factors that were related to successful classroom management:

1. withitness: the teacher knows what is going on in all parts of the room, all of the time.
2. overlapping: the teachers is able to deal with two or more activities at the same time.
3. smoothness: the teacher moves directly from one activity to the next without interrupting the flow of the class or the attention of the students.
4. momentum: the teacher is able to maintain the pace of the activities and make smooth, efficient transitions between activities.
5. accountability: the teacher is aware of the performance of all of the students, making sure they respond and providing feedback when it is necessary.
6. alerting: the teacher attempts to keep all of the students attentive all of the time.

   J. Kounin, *Discipline and Group Management in Classrooms* (New York: Holt, Rinehart and Winston, 1970).

[2] Robert M. W. Travers, "Empirically Based Teacher Education," in *Educational Forum* 39, no. 4 (May 1975): 417–433.

[3] The importance of animated performance in teaching is supported by the research of Rosenshine and Furst. They placed enthusiasm third in importance among teaching behaviors related to high student achievement. Much is gained when the teacher conveys commitment, excitement, and involvement with the subject matter. Barak Rosenshine and Norma Furst, "Enthusiastic Teaching: A Research Review," *School Review* 78, no. 4 (1979). Similarly, Cruickshank found that teachers who use appropriate gestures, eye contact, and verbal stimulation produce students who do better on tests than teachers who are generally uninspired and lackluster. Donald R. Cruickshank and Associates, *Teaching Is Tough* (Englewood Cliffs, N. J.: Prentice-Hall, 1980).

[4] A teacher-training study done by Gabrys has shown that this type of instruction with coaching can produce mastery of instructional strategies. In that study the teachers not only mastered new strategies, but these strategies became integrated in their day-to-day teaching performance and were visible ten weeks later in follow-up visits. R. Gabrys, "Training Teachers to Be Businesslike and Warm," paper presented at American Educational Research Association annual meeting, San Francisco, Apr. 1979 (Oneonta, N. Y.: SUNY, Oneonta, Department of Education).

CHAPTER 11

[1] The importance of having teachers combine a businesslike approach to

instruction with a strong affective focus has been reaffirmed by the results of two classroom research studies. In both cases teachers who were high on academic focus while maintaining a convivial, warm, and cooperative atmosphere had classrooms with much higher attention and greater achievement gain. N. Filby and L. Cahen, *Beginning Teacher Evaluation Study*, Phase III (San Francisco, Calif.: Far West Laboratory, 1977); and D. Solomon and A. J. Kendall, *Children in Classrooms* (New York: Praeger, 1979).

EPILOGUE

[1] Ernest L. Boyer, "Reflections on the Great Debate of '83," *Phi Delta Kappan* 65 (April 1984): 526.

[2] "The Paideia Proposal For School Reform," *Educational Leadership* 39 (May 1982): 579.

[3] D.E. Mitchell and C.T. Kerchner, *Collective Bargaining and Teacher Policy*, L.S. Shulman and G. Sykes, eds., *Handbook of Teaching and Policy* (New York: Longman, 1983).

[4] L.D. Hammond, A.E. Wise, and S.R. Pease, "Teacher Evaluation in the Organizational Context: A Review of the Literature," *Review of Educational Research* 53 (Fall 1983): 291.

[5] Karen Kepler Zumwalt, *Research on Teaching: Policy Implications for Teacher Education*, NSSE Yearbook, 1982 (Chicago, Ill.: University of Chicago Press), pp. 215–248.

[6] John I. Goodlad, "A Study of Schooling: Some Implications For School Improvement," *Phi Delta Kappan* 64 (April 1983): 553.

[7] Louis Rubin, ed., *The Inservice Education of Teachers: Trends, Processes, and Procedures*. (Boston: Allyn-Bacon, 1978), p. 309.

INDEX

ABOUT THE AUTHOR

LOUIS RUBIN has been active in teaching and learning for many years. He has served as a consultant to UNESCO, OECD, the National Institute of Education, the United States Office of Education, a number of foreign nations, and many state departments of education. Currently a professor of education at the University of Illinois (Champaign-Urbana), he is editor and author of a collection of books including: *Handbook on Curriculum; Educational Reform for a Changing Society; The Inservice Education of Teachers; The Future of Education; Facts and Feelings in the Classroom;* and *Critical Policy Issues in Education.* He has also taught at the University of California (Berkeley); the University of British Columbia; Stanford University; Simon Fraser University; and the University of Nebraska.

His professional interests focus on educational changes and innovation, the artistic aspects of teaching, and staff development. A widely-known speaker, he has lectured in Europe, Africa, Asia, and South America, as well as throughout the United States.